WILLIAM ALLEN WHITE OF EMPORIA

The Boss, Mr. White, Stops for a Minute at the Desk of His Managing Editor a Few Days before Christmas, 1940.

WILLIAM ALLEN WHITE
OF EMPORIA

by

FRANK C. CLOUGH
MANAGING EDITOR OF THE EMPORIA GAZETTE

New York   WHITTLESEY HOUSE   *London*

M C G R A W - H I L L   B O O K   C O M P A N Y ,   I N C .

010.92

C62w

WILLIAM ALLEN WHITE OF EMPORIA

Copyright, 1941, *by the* McGRAW-HILL BOOK COMPANY, INC.

18649

Feb. 1942

PUBLISHED BY WHITTLESEY HOUSE

A Division of the McGraw-Hill Book Company, Inc.

INTRODUCING FRANK CLOUGH

I HAVE NOT READ THIS BOOK. I DON'T know what is in it. Not a line has been submitted to me or to anyone closely connected with me or mine. So that when I open this book, it will all be new. I have no doubt some of it will seem strange and surprising; probably I shall bat my eyes with amazement here and there as I read its pages. But this also I surely know—that it will be an honest story and a picture of the *Gazette* and its environment as Frank Clough actually sees it.

For twenty years he has worked on this paper. He came with a note from his schoolteacher in Arkansas City saying that he was a bright boy and would like a job as college reporter. He was headed for one of our colleges. She also enclosed some clippings from the school paper or maybe manuscripts of his school essays. We took him on. He was college reporter then and he worked on Saturdays. In vacations he had a summer job. Finally we got him a full-time job and he was our star reporter. Later he went to Kansas City to see if he liked metropolitan journalism. He had been there a year or so when the country town in his blood called him home. And here he has been ever since. For a dozen years and more he has been in charge of the newsroom—which means that if he were on a larger paper, he would be managing editor. He is more than that with the *Gazette*.

Every morning by nine o'clock I try to have the editorial copy written and I put it on his desk. It mixes with the copy of the reporters and the telegraph and the neighbor-town news editors. Every line that I have written for *The Emporia Gazette* in the last dozen years has gone across his desk for copy-chopping and he has done a good job. Many a time he catches slips that I am making. Many a time he advises against this, that, or the other statement or position that he finds in the copy, and generally his word goes.

So I know that he is honest, discerning, and essentially kind in all his attitudes in life. I know that whatever he writes about me will describe me accurately as he has seen me, and more than likely, the picture that he makes of me will be the truth, however I may feel that he has either painted out the warts or overemphasized them! So here is the story and I hope, as you go forward, that you will enjoy it as much as I shall. For at least I can testify that it is a straight story from a good reporter.

WILLIAM ALLEN WHITE.

CONTENTS

CONTENTS

x

CONTENTS

INTRODUCTION

EVERY MAIL BRINGS TO THE OFFICE OF
The Emporia Gazette letters asking about William Allen White. They come from all parts of the United States and from foreign countries. They all want to know something about the editor of the daily newspaper in the Kansas country town who mixes in world affairs to the extent that he was named head of the national Committee to Defend America by Aiding the Allies. Does he live in Emporia and really edit a newspaper? If he is so prominent in world affairs, why does he stay in Kansas? What is his newspaper like? Does he actually work on the newspaper? Do you know him and does he spend any time in his newspaper office? What made him so well known? These are some of the questions addressed to the editor himself, to his secretary, and to members of his newspaper staff. They come from high school and college students assigned to write themes about him, to make class re-

ports on the editor, and to study his paper for journalism classes. They come from bankers, railroad workers, housewives, merchants, teachers, and lawyers. Since my name appears in newspaper directories as managing editor of Mr. White's paper, many of these letters come to me and I have answered hundreds of them. So, to answer those who are seeking definite facts and those who write merely out of curiosity, I have written the following story about "The Boss."

FRANK C. CLOUGH.

WILLIAM ALLEN WHITE
OF EMPORIA

CHAPTER I

NO WORK TODAY!

I PLACED THE TELEPHONE RECEIVER back on its hook at the end of my desk in the editorial room of *The Emporia Gazette* and chuckled. The boss, William Allen White, had just telephoned to say he was not coming down to the office that day and he was not going to do any work. I had heard that story many times before and I always got a good chuckle out of it. The boss always before, if he was in town, had come through with a good day's work and I knew this was not going to be any different.

The sports editor was tacking the summary on the end of a story he had written about a football game played the night before. The district editor had just placed on the copy hook for the printers a couple of dozen stories he had received in the morning mail from his neighbor-town correspondents. The telegraph editor still was going through his stack of copy of the night's happenings and picking out those stories on

3

which he expected further developments. Not one of the reporters had left the office to cover his morning run. It was nine o'clock on a typical Indian summer October morning in Kansas, and I was just as positive that the boss would come through with a good day's work as I was certain that I was going to get my weekly pay check that noon.

Before I had time to give any thought to the editorials for the day—whether to write some myself, see if someone else in the office had any ideas to get off his chest, or just use the reserve supply that Mr. White always keeps ahead for emergencies—in walked one of the office stenographers and handed me a dozen type-written pages.

"Here are the editorials for today," she said, just as she had done many times before. "I've been out to 'the house' and the boss dictated these and said he wasn't coming down and wasn't going to do any work today."

"Is he sick?" I asked, thumbing through the pages and finding a piece explaining why the editor believed Willkie and not Roosevelt should be elected; another stating clearly that Payne Ratner had made a good governor of Kansas and that he would be reelected without a doubt, for only twice in history had this state refused to give a Republican governor a second term; a third piece praising Emporia businessmen for the trade show being held in the new Civic Auditorium, and a fourth extolling the merit of Kansas weather.

"Well, he still has that cold he's had for a week and his voice seems to have gone back on him a little because he gave that talk out at the college yesterday and he looks tired, but I don't think he's sick. Mrs. White just told him he had to stay at home and rest up and he had me come out to the house instead of coming down here at eight o'clock."

"Was he in bed?" I asked.

"Oh, no, but his voice sounded as if he should've been. He had eaten breakfast and was out on the porch in the hammock reading the morning paper when I got there."

From that I knew what to expect when I went out to the house an hour and a half later with the editorial proofs for him to read. I did not even call to see if he wanted the proofs. If he was well enough to dictate the editorials, I knew he was well enough to want to make certain for himself that they were set properly in type. Also I knew that he would want to make some changes,

for, except in letters, seldom did he ever dictate anything that was exactly as he wanted it.

I knew before I went out to the house that I would
find him stretched out on his back in an old-fashioned
hammock, with his short, heavy body stretching the
netting to form a perfect pocket. He would have one
leg dangling from each side, the toes just able to
touch the floor. That was where one would always
find him when the weather was good. When the
weather was bad, one was just as certain to find him
buried deep in a low, overstuffed chair, his short legs
crossed in front of him and a book or paper in his
hand, held high but still low enough for him to look
over the top and see the wood fire in the big fireplace.

Just as he insists that a hammock is the only good
place to lounge in pleasant weather, the boss insists
that in front of the fire is the only place to sit in bad
weather. And a fireplace, in his mind, is not worth a
thing unless it is burning. When it was too cool for
comfort outside, yet too warm in the house for a big
fire, I have seen him put another log in the fireplace
and then open the windows so he would not be too
hot. And he insists on selecting his own logs for the
fire. Many times in the evening after dinner, when the
fire was blazing and there were half a dozen logs

stacked on the hearth ready for use, I have seen Mr. White leave the living room full of people while he went through the dining room and out a side door to a stack of wood piled close to the house. He had not liked the looks of the logs that were immediately available. And if I or one of the other men went out to help him with the wood, we always were waved away with, "Go on back, I know just what I want," or "You can close the door when I get in. I've got just the piece I need and I know where I want to put it."

A man who pipes gas into his fireplace is, in Mr. White's mind, in the same category as the family which has an antique chair that cannot be sat on, or some other piece of furniture originally designed for use but kept merely as an ornament.

But to get back to the man who was not going to do any work that day and had started by calling in a stenographer and before nine o'clock had written four editorials that would have been a full day's job for many editorial writers not nearly so well known over the country for their personal comments. Glancing through the living room from the front door, I could see the boss in his hammock on the south porch and Mrs. White sitting close to him in a large rocker, reading the *New York Times,* which had arrived that

7

morning by mail but had been printed two days before. Hundreds of times I had seen it just that way. If ever I were to find Mrs. White in the hammock and Mr. White in a rocker, I know I would pass out right on the spot. In fact, never have I seen anyone else in the hammock. Certainly I would not try to sit in it any more than I would slip into the pilot's place if I boarded a transcontinental air liner. I just would not belong. I have worked at his desk at the office, I have slept in his bed, and I have sat at his place in the big dining room and served when he was not there. Why, I do not know, but it would be sacrilegious to get into that hammock even if I were not afraid I would fall out of it.

When I walked out onto the broad porch, warm in the bright sunshine which filtered through the big elm trees, Mrs. White nodded and motioned me to a chair. Mr. White made no sign that he even saw me, although I had to crawl under one end of his hammock to get to the chair and I knocked my hat off doing it. I doubt if anything short of the hammock falling down would have attracted any attention from the boss, for, with a telephone in one hand and a receiver in the other, he was intent on a telephone conversation. A book he had been reading was spread open across his stomach. A pile of books and several bound printers' proofs of other books, not yet completed by the publishers, were on the floor beside the hammock, and I knew from that that Mr. White could not neglect his work even if he were sick. Those books were from the Book of the Month Club, of which he is a judge, and I knew without asking that he was reading them all—rushing through them in that particular way he has of seeming only to skim through them but actually getting more out of them than do most persons who read slowly.

"I thought he was sick," I remarked to Mrs. White quietly, so as not to interfere with the telephone conversation. At the office I have often heard him shout into the phone, "Hello! Hello! Hello!"—not just three times but dozens of times when he could not hear what was coming over the wire. Naturally that did not work, for the more he shouted the less he heard, and it usually ended with his calling to the operator at the switchboard in the next room, "Mary! I can't hear. Get me a new connection." I never knew how Mary worked it, but she always got it straightened out all right and Mr. White, who has patience with everything I have ever seen except a telephone, always got back on the line and finished his conversation. I have

9

never been afraid of the boss except when he has a telephone receiver at his ear, and then I give him a wide berth.

"He is sick," replied Mrs. White, much more softly than I had spoken, and I wondered if she felt about him as I did when he was at the telephone. "He had that awful cold and he just doesn't seem to get his strength back. He shouldn't have gone out to the college yesterday when the new president was inaugurated but he felt that he should. He has already talked to Washington and New York this morning and I think that's New York again. And he has to get these books read today and his report on them wired to New York by tonight. What's going on at the office? Is there any news of the war coming in over the Associated Press?"

"Good morning, young fellow, and what's the news with you this morning?" greeted Mr. White, clicking the receiver on the telephone and dropping it to the floor. "It's so nice of you to come out. I didn't have to see those proofs, but you know I always like to."

"Was that New York again?" asked Mrs. White.

I still had not had time to answer the questions of either of them about the news at the office.

"Yes," replied Mr. White, "it was New York again.

They say London had a pretty bad night again." And while he was saying it he had reached inside his top-coat and his suit coat and taken his fat, bright red fountain pen from his vest pocket and was already absorbed with his editorial proofs, his chin buried in the wool scarf wrapped around his neck, his white felt hat on backward and wadded up until it looked like a turban.

By "New York" I knew the Whites referred to the head office of the Committee to Defend America by Aiding the Allies. Nearly a year before, he had accepted the chairmanship of this national organization which felt that America was vulnerable to attack by the dictators of Europe and that the best defense for this continent was to help the Allies in their battle against Hitler. Since then Mussolini had joined Hitler, Belgium and France had fallen, and "the Allies" in the organization's name now meant Great Britain. Now it had become more apparent to Mr. White and his organization, which had grown rapidly until it had local organizations in most of the large cities in the United States and financial and moral supporters by the hundreds of thousands scattered across the country, that America must give all in its power to aid England.

11

I had heard a lot about this organization of men and women from all walks of life who felt that it was not only a humane thing to aid the enemies of the axis but that it also was the sensible way to defend America. The *Gazette* had printed the stories that came over the Associated Press wire about the committee's efforts to lift the embargo to permit sale of arms to the warring allies, and many of these stories contained statements by Mr. White, as the committee's head, which first had appeared as editorials in our own paper. Generally in the Associated Press stories we crossed out these statements of the boss's, but we never failed to carry the news of the committee's activities. I had heard Mr. White say that the committee needed money, but that it had to come in small gifts from individuals and he would not stand for big donations from manufacturers and munitions lords. He had taken the chairmanship, he explained to a group of us in the office one evening after the paper was out, because he believed in the cause, and he was not going to let the committee get in a position where anyone might accuse it of being a stooge for manufacturers who hoped to profit by the committee's work.

We around the office knew without his telling us that Mr. White got no salary as the committee's head.

We who knew about the financial affairs of the office knew that when the boss went to New York to a meeting of the committee, he tapped the *Gazette's* bank account for his expenses and paid his own freight. We also knew that the correspondence of the committee made so much more work that his one secretary, who usually worked only half a day, could not begin to keep up with letters that came in, all of which Mr. White answered. We had seen the girl, who had another job but who took the dictated editorials for an hour every morning, spending more time with Mr. White and less with her other job. We also had seen another full-time stenographer put on the *Gazette's* pay roll to work mostly for the Committee to Defend America by Aiding the Allies. The only thing we had seen him get out of the committee was when still another secretary was needed early in the summer and the committee had sent out a girl who had been working in the New York office but had gone to her home in Illinois on a vacation. Instead of reporting back to New York, the committee sent her to Emporia for a month.

Most of us around the *Gazette* office are accustomed to hard work, and anyone who was in the office much could easily understand how we got into the habit. It

13

has been a natural trait of the office, set by the boss. This summer, for instance, here was a man seventy-two years old, heading one of the busiest committees in the country, reading and reporting on a huge stack of books every month for the Book of the Month Club, covering the Republican and Democratic national conventions for a large newspaper syndicate, writing political articles for magazines and newspapers, making several school commencement speeches as well as frequent radio and meeting addresses for the defense committee, taking an active part in national Republican politics as well as serving as local committeeman from the Second Precinct of the Fourth Ward on the Republican county committee, writing two columns of editorials every day, and still having time to enjoy his home, read half a dozen newspapers every day, see a movie about once a week, and entertain dinner guests from two to four times a week. And then in his spare time he has kept an eye on all the local news in the paper, reorganized the business office, seen to it that the wage and hour law was being observed, and attended Rotary Club every Tuesday noon, after each meeting telling the chef what the club was to be served next Tuesday. Chairman of the Rotary menu committee is one of his favorite jobs.

And with all this, Mr. White is no ball of fire. He works hard but quietly, and never a day passes but he walks through the office and talks to the boys in the back shop and pressroom, as well as the people in the offices. And rarely does he fail to look at two or three dozen other Kansas newspapers every day to see how they are printing the news and advertising in comparison with the *Gazette* and to see what other Midwestern editorial writers are saying.

I would not want to make Mr. White look like a superman. He would kick my desk out from under me if I did. But he does get a lot of things done. To understand how he does the things he does, one must know about his early life, for he did not start in all at once trying to see how much he could do. Not only must one know about Mr. White's early life, but he should also know something of his parents to understand how the Kansas editor does what he does and why he does it.

CHAPTER II

LUCK PLAYS A HAND

IN THE FIRST PLACE, MR. WHITE BELIEVES that luck or getting the breaks has played an important part in his life. At least he believes that luck started him in the newspaper business.

In May of 1885, when Mr. White was a student at the College of Emporia, he decided that it was not fitting and proper for his mother to support him in school. His father had died and his mother was keeping boarders in their home town, El Dorado, to support herself and send her only son to school. Near the close of his freshman year, he wrote three letters to El Dorado—one to George Tolle, who ran a grocery store; one to Cass Friedburg, who had a dry goods store, and the other to T. P. Fulton, publisher of the *El Dorado Democrat*. He asked each of them for a job, not just for the summer vacation, but as something permanent so that he might help his mother.

"Tolle and Friedburg knew my desultory ways and

16

Mr. and Mrs. White and Son, W. L. White, on the Porch When
"Young Bill" Visited His Parents in the Spring of 1941.

rejected my job suggestion," Mr. White related many years later. "T. P. Fulton knew my father and took a chance."

On May 30, 1885, the *El Dorado Democrat* printed the following news item:

"Will A. White will take a position on the *Democrat* June 1st."

But it was far from a position, and when young White reported for work he was told to take off his coat and roll up his sleeves. If he had had any idea that he was to become a writer and sit behind a desk, it was dispelled now, for Fulton led the boy into the print shop where he told the foreman, the foreman's son, and the apprentice that here was the new printer's devil. The new boy was given all the little jobs to do around the country print shop and it was dirty work. While learning to set type, feed paper into the big press which printed the newspaper, and operate the job presses on which handbills, calling cards, stationery, and sales bills were printed, the new boy was assigned to sweep out the shop and office every day, keep the windows clean, and run the errands. After he had been there a short time, they began to let him go up and down the main street gathering local items for the paper, which he never wrote as the regular reporter did. Because he was learning the type cases and how to make up a paper, young White came in off the street, went right through the office to the print shop, and set up his news in type. Often when the boss went fishing, White was allowed to clip editorials from other papers, get them into type, and make up the *Democrat's* editorial page. As he assumed responsibility, the editor, who would rather fish or talk politics with his friends around the courthouse and up and down the main street, let White do some of the collecting from the merchants who had not paid their advertising bills. He would deliver the stationery and sales bills and try to collect for them when he delivered.

"When the editor was out of town and I did the collecting, I would knock down the money he owed me," I have heard Mr. White say. "I always got my pay."

His first editorial writing came in the winter of 1886, when the editor of the *Democrat* was in Washington. He also got up most of the local news and, only about six months after he had started in the business, generally was responsible for getting out the paper.

Not long ago I asked Mr. White if he thought he

ever would have amounted to anything if he had landed a job in the grocery or the dry goods store instead of the newspaper.

"I haven't any idea," he admitted frankly. "But I know I never would have had as much fun out of life as I've had around the newspaper office."

I would bet my best shirt that he would have been a total flop in the dry goods store, for clothes seemingly mean little to him. He knows values and he buys good merchandise but he gives little thought to what he wears or how he wears it. He might not have been this way had he got into the mercantile business, but the fact that he always has been so much more interested in what people do than in how they look makes me believe that Cass Friedburg, the El Dorado dry goods man, did Mr. White a favor when he failed to answer the application for a job.

Mr. White wears good clothes and cleanliness seems to be second nature. I have never seen him without a freshly laundered shirt every day, even when he was vacationing in the mountains and loafing around his cabin. His dry-cleaning bill is terrific. In fact, his cleaning bill always is more than his cleaner's bill for advertising in the *Gazette* and the cleaners are good advertisers in Emporia. The boss can get his vest but-

19

toned up crooked, he can go around with his suit coat collar turned up in the back or one of the cuffs on his pants turned wrong side out, and it never seems to bother him. Wearing his battered hats backward seems to come natural to him. But I have never seen him without a necktie. Once I went to the house and found him sitting up in bed reading, wearing pajamas and a bright red necktie. Red is his favorite color and he likes to express it in his ties. The nearer they come to matching the scarlet fountain pen he carries in his vest pocket, the better he seems to like them. A red tie seems to do something for him, and nearly always when he comes downtown after being "under the weather" at home for a few days he wears a flaming tie.

Mr. White might have made a good grocer. Certainly he would have been better at that than in the dry goods business, for next to people, food interests him more than anything else. He plays no golf, he cannot drive an automobile, and he seldom goes to baseball or football games or other sporting events. Once I attended a wrestling match with him, when the nationally famous Strangler Lewis tangled on the mat with Clarence Jenkins, a local policeman who was gaining some fame as a grappler. Mr. White knew

Jenkins, who for a time had the assignment of coming into the *Gazette* office at four o'clock every morning and lighting the fires under the metal pots so that the linotype machines would be hot for the operators at seven thirty. The afternoon of the match, the Strangler, who also is a lawyer, came into the office to meet Mr. White. They had a pleasant conversation and the wrestler knew something of the books he saw piled on the editor's desk. I know Mr. White went to the match only to see what there was to wrestling that made a man like Lewis earn his living that way. I have gone to football games with the boss, when we were away from home at an editorial meeting and the editors were guests of the state university athletic department, but he never paid any attention to the game. He spent most of the time watching the crowd. The apples he always bought from the student venders, which always chapped your lips and face in the cool, fall weather, had more interest for him than did the actual game.

With food as one of his main interests, he might have gone far in the grocery business had Mr. Tolle of El Dorado needed a clerk or a delivery boy when Mr. White applied for a job in 1885. The fact that he has refused the presidency or any other office in the Rotary Club but takes great delight in being the chair-

21

man and only member of the menu committee makes me believe that, if Mr. White had become a grocery clerk, the people of El Dorado would eventually have had an excellent grocer who would have influenced their eating habits just as he, as an editor, has influenced the thoughts of his readers.

"Food interests me," Mr. White wrote in the *Rotarian* magazine, the editor of which had written to ask why a nationally known editor took delight in preparing the menus for the Rotary Club members. "My father, a country doctor, kept a hotel for a few years while I was a boy in my early teens. I used to go to market with him.

"Before I began to study algebra, I knew, therefore, where the sirloin cut lay in a beef carcass, the difference between a T-bone steak and a round. Before I could 'bound' Kansas I knew how to pick out a rib roast and the essentials of a rump roast. Before I was fifteen I knew that a steak to be really edible should never be cooked with any water or fat in the skillet and that it should be cut an inch and a half or two inches thick and seared in a red-hot skillet on both sides, then turned every two or three minutes until it was done.

"I also knew how to make biscuits and pancakes as

a boy. My parents had a wide dietary range and I was compelled to eat what was set before me. Otherwise it was left cold for me for the next meal.

"So I learned to like many kinds of foods and to eat the glands of the animals, the liver, the sweetbreads, the brains, the kidneys, and the tripe. Headcheese was my delight. Every kind of vegetable known to the Temperate Zone I have enjoyed for fifty years and more—even broccoli! I don't balk at parsnips nor oyster plant!

"When I was a young man in my early twenties, in Kansas City, Missouri, working on the *Kansas City Journal,* I had to 'board out' a trade account in a big, first-class, fashionable hotel, and there, being gastronomically devilish, I ate everything on the wide bill of fare in the early nineties that the great American world afforded in food. I learned to like everything. The philandering which an ardent nature naturally would enjoy, I have had to turn to a wide and catholic daily taste in food. So monogamy has not been, with me, a cheerless chore. I have had other physical interests, chiefly gastronomic. Here, by the way, is the basic secret of the matrimonial proverb that the way to a man's heart is through his stomach. I never knew a

23

woman-chasing man whose wife was a good and adventurous cook."

The Rotary Club meets every Tuesday noon and the seventy-six members have a sixty-cent meal in a hotel which has average food and little or no imagination in its regular menu. But Mr. White, as Rotary menu chairman, has made the Rotary luncheons something that, if served to the regular customers, might either make the hotel known far and wide among connoisseurs of food or might drive away the regular customers. He once went forty-six weeks without repeating a menu. He has served ragouts and sea foods à la Newburg, even with a little sherry in them. He has had oysters, meat stews of all kinds, pigs' feet, New England boiled dinners, and once he put a soufflé over on them. He makes them eat onions, green peppers, garlic, and horse-radish. He even tried jellied consommé on them once and they ate it.

"Eat it; it's good," says Mr. White when he springs something new on the men, who, by nature and the general Kansas way of living, are meat, mashed potatoes, and gravy men. The men eat it, and sometimes it is good and sometimes it is not so good. Mr. White never knows, for he does not eat it himself. Always at noon, whether at home or away, his luncheon consists of two pieces of whole-wheat toast, a bowl of milk, coffee with an equal amount of hot milk, and some stewed fruit or melon.

"I guess it's all right," sighed an insurance man, after a Rotary meal of lamb stew with onions, carrots, and turnips, "but I'd like to see him eat it once himself."

What the Rotarians do not know is that, at home in the evening, the White family dinner consists not only of the comparatively few more or less unusual things that the boss has served at Rotary, but also of special dishes the Whites have learned about in their travels all over the world. Many a *Gazette* employee who grew up believing that beef or pork, steak or roast well done, potatoes, and gravy were the only things good to eat, has learned to appreciate dishes made by recipes the Whites have brought from France, China, Russia, and the many other countries in which they have traveled.

One of Mr. White's favorite delicacies, which few other persons like, even in the Middle West, where they are common, is the pawpaw, a bananalike fruit which grows on a tree and after frost turns brown. A half dozen of them in a closed room smell to most persons like a carload of overripe bananas. But Mr. White

25

thinks they are great, and every fall—sometimes even before the first frost—he writes a short editorial for his paper calling attention to the pawpaw season. And sure enough, as soon as the fruit is ripe, several farmers pick them along the creeks and bring them in to the *Gazette*—gifts for the editor.

Someone last fall left several dozen of them in a box on Mr. White's desk while he was out of town. Late that afternoon he returned, about the time the office was beginning to smell like a fruit room someone had abandoned. Stopping in his office on my way home, to ask the boss about his trip to Chicago to a meeting of a committee of the American Society of Newspaper Editors, I found him loading into his arms half a dozen books, a stack of newspapers, and the box of pawpaws.

"Do you really like to eat those things?" I asked.

"And I'll show you how," he replied quickly, dumping his load onto his desk, breaking a particularly ripe pawpaw in the middle and squeezing the meat of the fruit from the skin into his mouth. "I'll tell you a little secret. All Negroes but a very few white men like these."

"Okay," I agreed. "Can I give you a ride home?"

"No, thanks, but you can help me out to the car

26

with these things," he answered, handing me some
books and the box of fruit.

He paused on the front steps to talk with a passer-by,
and, as I walked to the car, the Negro chauffeur, a
young fellow who drives for Mr. and Mrs. White only
when they go out of town, got out of the car and
offered to take the things from me.

"Oh, oh!" he exclaimed, as he smelled the pawpaws.

"Don't eat 'em," I warned, remembering Mr.
White's conversation inside the office.

"Don't worry," he said, quickly putting the box in
the back seat and taking a few brisk steps away. "Pawpaws are one thing I couldn't eat any more than I
could avocadoes."

Mr. White's ability to appreciate food as more than
something just to satisfy the appetite and fill the stomach makes me believe he might have been a good grocer and his influence might have been wide. But just
as he has a good time with food, he has a good time
with his newspaper. He makes work a pleasure and he
is never too busy to wisecrack or even make a pun or
two, these probably the outgrowth of the practical
jokes he enjoyed when he was a printer.

CHAPTER III

FUN IN A PRINT SHOP

THE COLLEGE BOY WHO STARTED WORK
as a printer's devil in 1885 to help support himself and his mother did not believe that life should
be all serious. Ewing Herbert, who now publishes a
daily newspaper in Hiawatha, Kans., went to work as
printer in El Dorado about the time White was beginning to spend some time reporting, writing the
editorials, and handling some of the business affairs.
Although he and White were about the same age,
Herbert was a regular printer and he knew the ways
of a country print shop.

"I remember how once I showed him type lice,"
Herbert related years later. "White was nearsighted
and bent very close, at my suggestion, to see the almost
invisible insects. As I slapped the type together and
saw the dirty water streaming from his face I did not
laugh according to plans and specifications. The joke
had lost its flavor on the instant and I felt a hearty

contempt for myself for foolishly betraying one deserving of better treatment. I begged his pardon and implored him to squirt dirty water in my face—yes, throw a bucketful on my person. He called my bluff and did all I asked and more. It was a mad afternoon we had of it, for, when the water buckets had been emptied, we flung the sponge and towels at each other so long as they hung together; and when they gave out, we bought watermelons, ate what we liked, and threw the scraps at citizens who passed the office, which was very wrong, of course, for it cost our employer more than it did either of us."

From then on Herbert and White, both of whom later went to Emporia to work, became warm friends. In recent years they have seen each other seldom, but each continues to read the other's paper. Herbert became editor of *Kansas Newspaperdom,* the official publication of the Kansas Editorial Association, in 1894, which was before White had attracted any prominence at all outside Kansas and not much within his home state. In the first issue of the little pamphlet, Herbert printed White's photograph on the first page, showing the young Kansas editor wearing a dress coat, boiled shirt, stand-up collar, and white tie. I believe the few remaining copies of the first issue of *Kansas News-*

paperdom are the only prints of that picture in existence. Certainly there is none hanging around the *Gazette* office or the White home. In the twenty years I have known Mr. White I have seen him on special occasions in Emporia wear a dinner jacket, which he still calls a tuxedo, but I have never seen him in white tie and tails, although I know he has them for special occasions when he goes East. Only once, by his own admission, has he ever worn a silk hat and that was when he attended a formal dinner party in New York when his son, William L. "Young Bill" White, happened to be there at the same time.

"I didn't want to wear that plug hat, but Bill insisted," said the father, when he came home. "I never wore a silk hat before in my life and I guess Bill knew it, because he certainly was careful of that hat, which he had bought when he attended Harvard. We left our hotel together and Bill, who wasn't even going to the party, insisted on going over with me in the taxi to be a nursemaid to the hat. He let me wear it down in the elevator, through the lobby, and onto the street, but then he grabbed it like a man catching an egg. He knew I would forget to duck when I got in the taxi and would break the hat, so I went bareheaded across town and Bill put the hat back on my head as I entered the hotel for the party. I thought sure he would be on the sidewalk waiting—for the hat, not me—when the party was over, but he wasn't. I carefully carried the thing back to our hotel and I hope I never have to wear one of them again."

Along with the picture, Herbert printed in the little newspaper association magazine of 1884 a sketch of the life of young White and made the prediction: "I am certain that his present success is but a shadow of that which the coming years will deliver him."

Few people today know that Mr. White ever wrote poetry, but in the early days, like most young writers, he tried his hand at verse. Herbert, in praising his fellow Kansan, published a poem which White had written several years before, when he was learning the newspaper business in El Dorado. Titled "Shorty," White had written the following tribute to a printer:

> My stock of heroes never wuz
> So very big, you see, becuz
> I never understood the plan
> 'at they are built on, an' a man
> Don't like to keep things 'round that he
> Can't predicate, at least that's me
> All over an' that's why, you know,
> I got to liking Shorty so.

31

He wa'n't no hero, Shorty wa'n't,
Jes' a ornery tall slim gaunt
Ol' print 'at loaft around the den
An' read exchanges, working when
Some print upstairs 'u'd want to quit
An' take a lay off from his sit.
He wa'n't so awful extra though
At stickin' type—a little slow
Perhaps because he wuzn't pat
At soljerin' the hook fer phat.

And pore? Well, now, you're talkin' right;
He was the dernest looking sight
Regarding clothes you ever saw;
Last year's bird-nest wouldn't draw
Wu'th a cent 'gin Shorty's show.
Shorty's wife was diff'rent though:
Jes' as different from him,
Plump and short as he was slim:

Brisk and lively too, I guess,
Yet I bet the lovinges'
Girl you find in any state—
Shorty thought so't any rate:
"My ol' woman," Shorty'd say,
In a lovin', tender way,
'at 'u'd do a man more good
Than a dozen sermons would.

Shorty never paid to go
To any circus, fair or show,
He just 'u'd show his rule and smile,
Wink and walk in slick as ile.

Some People Might Think This Desk Is Cluttered Up, but Mr. White Doesn't. He Knows Everything That's on It. And He Knows Exactly Where to Find It—If He Looks Long Enough.

An' so I bet when Shorty dies
An' hits the road for Paradise
His golden rule'll pass him through
Jes' like his other used to do.

William Allen White has lived in Kansas all but
two of his seventy-three years, and by far the greatest
part of his life has been spent in Emporia. He was
born in Emporia, then a town of only a few hundred
people, on Feb. 10, 1868. Although the house in which
he was born is gone, Mr. White owns the lot, and on
it is a modern, two-story brick building, leased to an
automobile agency. His parents were Dr. Allen White
and Mary Ann Hatton White. His father's people
originally lived in Massachusetts, the family record
going back to Nicholas White, the Emporia editor's
great grandfather. John White, son of Nicholas White,
married Fear Perry, who, according to the family tra-
dition, was a sister or an aunt of Commodore Perry—
Mr. White frankly admits he does not know which.
The grandparents left Massachusetts and lived in
Ohio, where Dr. Allen White was born.

CHAPTER IV

COUNTRY DOCTOR-
STOREKEEPER

M R. WHITE'S FATHER CAME TO LYON
County to live in 1859. At first he practiced
medicine, but after a few years he established a general store in Emporia—one of those old-fashioned
country stores that handled everything the early settlers might need and sold them in large quantities, for
in those days the farm families came to town seldom
and, when they did come in, they bought enough to
last for a long time.

William Hammond, a pioneer of this country who
died a few years ago, loved to tell the story of how
Dr. Allen White, the merchant, once was taken in.
The Soden mill was the only flour mill in Emporia at
that time and Dr. White and Soden had had words.
White flatly announced he would sell no more of
Soden's flour, but would import his supply, although
there was no railroad running into Emporia and all

34

materials brought there had to come by overland stage. Hammond, a boy then, was going with his father to Leavenworth, nearly a hundred miles away on the Missouri River, to get supplies, and Dr. White gave the operator of the big freight wagon, drawn by several teams of horses, a large order for flour. It took the freighter nearly two weeks to make the trip, carrying a load of Soden's flour to Leavenworth and bringing back a supply of general merchandise. When the wagon returned to Emporia and the driver began to unload at White's store, it was discovered that the Leavenworth dealer had filled Dr. White's order with some of the same Soden flour that the wagon had hauled to Leavenworth.

"He hollered his head off, but there wasn't anything he could do about it," the younger Hammond used to say, when he would come into the *Gazette* office and tell the story years later. "Old Doc White sold the flour, but he didn't do it cheerfully. And he wouldn't have sold it at all, but he didn't have any other kind to sell."

Recently Kansas newspapers carried a little feature called "Jaywisers," worked up by an organization to advertise the Jayhawker state. One of the questions in the feature was: "Who was Dr. Allen White?" The answer was: "The father of William Allen White and the mayor of El Dorado."

Joseph M. Satterthwaite, one of Kansas's oldest editors and now editor of the *Douglass Tribune,* a weekly paper published in a small town near Wichita, read the "Jaywiser" and was indignant at the brief sentence given as the answer. Satterthwaite had known Dr. White during the early days in El Dorado.

"The answer was correct as far as it went, but to Butler County and to El Dorado, in particular, the reply was meager indeed," Satterthwaite wrote. "For had it not been for Dr. Allen White, Butler County would not have been as it is and El Dorado would have been rubbed off the map.

"Well, Dr. Allen White came to El Dorado when the real life first started in that town in 1869. (William Allen White was a year old then.) He had been a few years in Kansas, residing in Lyon County. He built for himself, his wife, and his little yearling son a native lumber frontier house on the site where the government post office now stands. He built, stocked, and operated a drugstore on Main Street, four lots south of the principal corner.

"He was the most public-spirited citizen in the new town started out of the wilds, with Emporia, sixty miles distant, the nearest railroad station, and even Emporia a frontier town.

"It was important that a live, starting town in a new county must have a newspaper. Dr. White led off in getting one, and T. B. Murdock, an Emporia printer, and J. S. Danford, an adventurer disposed to speculation, were subsidized by the El Dorado businessmen to get a Washington hand press and supply of type from Cincinnati and start the *Walnut Valley Times* in the winter of 1869-1870. We think that Murdock and Danford were given $1,000 by the El Dorado businessmen to come and start the paper.

"When contributions were raised for public enterprises, then the name of Dr. White always headed the list with the largest contribution.

"In the early seventies El Dorado was sitting pretty, near the center of a big county into which a flood of immigration was pouring. But stormy conditions soon gathered. A territory twenty miles wide on the south end of the county had been ceded to settlers by the Osage Indians. For the accommodation of this immigration a new land office for filings was located at Augusta. That land office drew all the settlers there to file on their claims. Land office attorneys and real estate agents flocked there. Augusta boomed. It purposed to divide the county and make for itself the county seat of the south county, and from then on came the all-absorbing tug of a county-seat war.

"El Dorado had to have a courthouse to give it advantage in holding the county seat. It had not the popular strength to vote taxation upon the county to build a $2,000 building. Private contributions by men interested in El Dorado must pay for the structure. Dr. Allen White's name headed the list of contributors.

"Fight after fight followed. Railroad bond propositions to give El Dorado or Augusta an advantage were promulgated. County-seat elections and the choice of representatives in the legislature followed, wave upon wave.

"Politics, and fitness for office, all things of public nature were submerged beneath the all-absorbing county-seat fight. Nor did it stop there; private bitterness and personal animosities naturally sprouted and grew. At one time and for quite a while both Augusta and El Dorado had armed organizations to carry out their purposes. It is a marvel that actual battle did not result," Satterthwaite concluded.

"As a matter of fact," added William Allen White, reprinting the Satterthwaite piece in the *Gazette,* "a battle almost occurred one summer night when Augusta came armed to storm the courthouse by force and found El Doradoans, forewarned, packed inside the courthouse and over its roofs with rifles sticking out of the windows and doors and bristling from the roof like 'quills upon the fretful porcupine.' Augusta accepted the inevitable and retired, nursing its wrath. But 'old Doc White'—he was called old Doc, though he was only in his fifties, by the young veterans of the Civil War, homesteaders with their pretty young wives—old Doc, a shining target in white nankeen pants, white pleated shirt, and white Panama hat, paraded the streets around the courthouse, the only unarmed man in the town, to greet the invaders with gay and flippant persiflage. His wife begged him to put on his black Sunday suit to be less conspicuous, but he was ribald in his reply that if they hit him they wouldn't hit the courthouse! And his wife was frightened to what now we know as the jitters. Augusta stood around for an hour looking at the courthouse fortress and went home and burned old Doc in effigy, head of 'the Courthouse Ring'! It gave him delight to his dying days. For he was so built that he loved better than the applause of the multitude, the impotent cackling rage of his enemies. At that he could

39

chuckle. He smiled at the memory of that hour on his deathbed."

But to get on with Editor Satterthwaite's story:

"El Dorado's part, and through that the county's part, was managed by what was then termed a 'Ring.' This Ring was composed of about a dozen public-spirited businessmen of El Dorado. Dr. Allen White was the head of that Ring. He did not seek that distinction for himself, but his wisdom, his loyalty to El Dorado, and his generosity naturally put him there. He sought nothing for himself. The warfare was well over when he was made mayor of El Dorado. His fitting place was that of 'the power behind the throne.'

"He was an ardent Democrat, but party politics had no place or part with him so long as the interests of El Dorado were at issue. The county was overwhelmingly Republican, and he, like Samson of old, felt that it was wise to use the Republican heifer to plow for El Dorado. When county-seat matters subsided, he did his part to organize the Democratic party in the county. He contributed liberally to get a Democratic paper in El Dorado, but of short-lived success.

"We could say much more. He built the nicest home in the city. He built it for a home, and had no inclination to make of it a public house. But El Do-

40

rado badly needed a good hotel. In those days when 'drummers' were the life of trade, a good hotel was a great asset to any town. They sought the best hotels in the country and paid their way. For the houses that sent them out paid their expenses. And they learned from each other where the best hotels were. So, Dr. White opened that home-intended building for a hotel, not for personal gain but at a personal sacrifice, that the town he loved so well might be benefited.

"Mrs. Jesse Stratford is writing a history of Butler County. That history will be incomplete if the part taken by Dr. Allen White in the early settlement of the county is not fittingly recorded there.

"El Dorado should build him a monument and dedicate it to the county whose entirety he preserved."

CHAPTER V

HIS MOTHER WAS A "CAPTAIN"

WILLIAM ALLEN WHITE'S MOTHER was the first child of Irish immigrants who came to America a few months before she was born in 1830. She lived to be nearly ninety-five years old and was a strong character. She lived with her son and his family for a short time after Mr. White came to Emporia and purchased *The Emporia Gazette,* but she loved her independence and, although she had her own room and could do as she pleased, she preferred her own home. For many years, until her death on May 6, 1924, she lived in a large, old-fashioned, brick house next door to that of her son. Physically, Mr. White looks like his mother. He does not look his seventy-three years and she appeared to be much younger than she was. The influence of both his mother and his father is shown in the editor's character and it would be difficult to say if he took after one more than the other.

42

The day after his mother's death, Mr. White wrote, as an editorial for the *Gazette,* a story of her life, which reveals much of his boyhood days.

"My mother was the type of woman known as a 'captain'—a masterful person who had her own ideas, and being purebred Irish always wanted to make her own views prevail," he wrote. "It is that spirit which from time immemorial has made the Irish the rulers of the world. She was left an orphan when she was sixteen, with two younger children—her brother and her sister—to rear. The brother ran away and went to sea on a Lake Erie boat, and her sister got married, so my mother, being footloose, devoted herself to the passion of her life—education. She learned the dressmaking trade and still later the milliner's trade, all to keep herself in school. She fell in with friends who took her from the town of her childhood—Oswego, N. Y.—to Chicago. There she heard of a coeducational college at Galesburg, Ill., where she went in the early fifties. She must have been very happy there; for as a child I learned of the glories of Knox College, and it came to be a place of high adventure to me, a sort of port of dreams. In the meantime her sister, who had married, began to have babies, and my mother's school record shows that every other year for nearly

43

ten years she was out of school helping her sister with her babies.

"During the Civil War my mother taught school in southern Illinois, in a town where the families of the Union officers were quartered. And in 1865, hearing of the opening of the Kansas State Normal School at Emporia, she started out to get more education. She rode in on the stage. . . . She wanted to enter school here but could find no place to room, so she went to Council Grove (a smaller town about thirty miles northwest of Emporia) and taught school, defying the school board and the sentiment of the town by inviting the Negro children to attend. She was just that kind. She was thirty-five years old and was a black abolitionist Republican. Sam Wood, a dear and unfettered old free-state adventurer, took her case up, stood by her, and made it possible for the colored children to have their school. The next year she met my father at a dance in the Robinson House here in Emporia, when she was teaching school in Cottonwood Falls (another small town twenty miles west of Emporia, in the cattle country). He was a dozen years older than she, in his late forties, and their love affair was pretty mature and deliberate probably. But a baby was coming in the sister's family so my mother went back to Michigan to help her with it, and in a few months my father went after her and they were married—she thirty-seven and he forty-eight.

"I was born just a year after their marriage and a year after that my father, who was a natural pioneer, found Emporia growing too sophisticated and crowded, so he pulled out for El Dorado in the Walnut Valley with his family. El Dorado in that day was a tough town. Emporia never was. My mother stood it, but she disliked it. The shooting and drinking and sporting around were not what she had bargained for in life when she spent ten years getting a college education when most women are having their love affairs and babies. But she brought books into the rough little town, and my earliest memory is of her reading to me. She was one of the women who helped to found the city library in the mid-seventies and when I was a little child she gave me books for mature minds. Before I was twelve she had read most of Dickens to me, and 'Middlemarch' and 'Adam Bede' and one of George Sand's novels which I have never been able to locate; but it was raw meat for a boy. But still good for me. Scott and Charles Reade and Wilkie Collins were read before my teens were well started and after that I went alone.

"But in the meantime my father, who had been a country doctor and a country merchant, and had always dabbled in real estate and had made money easily and so had a light opinion of it, decided that he would be a gentleman farmer. He bought a big farm, built a log house on it, with a big fireplace and all of the foolish trappings of a pioneer farmer's place in the early part of the last century—the kind of a place in which he was born and reared. He could as well have had a decent board and plastered house with fairly comfortable appointments. But no—he wanted to reproduce the good old days. I was only a child then but I remember what an awful family row started over that fake farm adventure. My mother could get no hired girl to go to the farm, and the loft was full of hired men; for my father in his fifties couldn't farm. He even built me a trundle bed to go under the big log bed, and that made work and when my mother blew up—well, we moved back to town and the men had a great joke on my father. Men were supposed to run their own homes in those days—but not men who married my mother. She was, as I say, what is called a captain.

"When we got back to town, my father, who was one of those hospitable, expansive souls, was forever inviting people in to stay with him. He built a whaling big house—for the seventies—ten rooms, and kept it full of company. This also was not to my mother's liking, and I remember she was always telling him we were going to the poorhouse with so much company. So what did he do but open a hotel. And certainly there was a mad woman. She loved to cook, but she had to have the best. And he had to have the best and that meant thick beefsteak and rare roast beef, and throwing everything away but the breasts from the prairie chickens, and real buckwheat cakes that you stir and leave on the reservoir of the stove to rise overnight to serve with real maple syrup in the morning. And all for $2 a day! The help wouldn't stay and my mother had all the work to do. She saw we were losing money—and little my father cared. For he would swank round the front porch in his nankeens, his white vest, and his white suspenders, talking politics, while my mother used to sweat in the kitchen and complain that we were headed straight for the poorhouse. In passing, let me say that the only real economy my father ever practiced was this: he kept his high-priced, fine-cut tobacco in a silver case in his hip pocket and carried plug tobacco in his coat pocket for strangers. Then one day, she blew up again, and the hotel closed. She was right. But it broke my father's heart. Keeping hotel and losing money at it, so that he could not accuse himself of capitalizing his hospitality, was the one proud period in his life. The money he made in real estate—and he was really a sharp trader and had a good nose for values—he put in the hotel. So we really were not much poorer when we quit. But quitting hurt his pride a bit. The men had another laugh on him.

"My mother always wanted two things—a watch and an operation. My father had his pride. He said she had a good clock and never was out of the home, so what did she need of a watch, and being a doctor he knew perfectly well that she did not need an operation. So these desires were repressed. I was fourteen when he fell sick and died—died largely of a broken heart. He was a Democrat, but a prohibitionist, and when his party turned down John Martin—known as Gentleman John—at Topeka, who would not run on the nullification platform for governor, and when the party nominated Glick and ran him on the nullification platform, my father, a delegate to the convention, came home, went to bed, and died. He died Thursday. We had the funeral Saturday. He was mayor of El Dorado and the funeral was in every way satisfactory

48

The Emporia Editor at the Age of Five in His First "Store-bought" Suit.

to the Irish heart of my mother. Sunday it was lonely in the house with the kin all gone. So Monday she took me by the hand and led me downtown and bought the best lady's watch in El Dorado. (Mr White has carried the watch since his mother's death. It now is more than fifty-five years old and keeps good time.)

"In a few weeks she was planning for an operation. But when I cried and begged her not to leave me an orphan, she sighed and gave it up, thus passing within a few weeks of glorious freedom from the tyranny of one man to that of another. She held me, however, to an education. Her life's passion rose and a naturally unstudious son was crammed through high school into college. She moved to Lawrence to be with him in the state university. And she kept fairly well abreast of him and renewed her youth. But her freedom was gone. She still walked on her heels and made a great show of having her own way, but she surrendered to her maternal love.

"For nearly thirty years she had lived in this town (Emporia), most of the time in her own house and always in her own way. Any kind of fetters galled her. The Irish love of freedom ruled her soul. She was sentimental to a fault. When Grover Cleveland was first elected in 1884, her husband was dead. But she knew

49

he would rejoice, so with grim loyalty holding back
her tears of rage at the elevation of a Democrat to the
presidency, this black Republican abolitionist put a
lighted candle in every window of her home when the
news of Cleveland's victory came. Then she went to
the back of the house where she could not be seen
when the Democratic parade came around. It shamed
her, but she was proud of her shame. She was always
like that, and so often was most unhappy, having small
sense of humor. As the years came upon her she had
grown more and more grim, more and more doleful
at the restraints of life. She has had a long journey—
nearly ninety-five years of it, yearning passionately for
a freedom that she could never quite define. So it is
with all of us, in our heart of hearts. And yesterday
she had release—into the world of truth, into the land
where our visions blurred by the earth's dull circum-
spection come true and satisfy the soul. I am sure, and
so I am most happy that whatever survives of my
mother today is young and free and happy beyond
human words. For the iron that bound her heart
chafes her no longer. She is the captain of her soul."

CHAPTER VI

THE BOY TURNS MAN

MR. WHITE'S BOYHOOD DAYS WERE NO different from those of the average small-town Kansas boy at that time, except, interested in books by his mother when he was very young, he did more reading than most boys on the plains of the prairie state. While he was attending the grade schools and high school in El Dorado, he went swimming in the Walnut River, where the water was deep and where the wild grapevines grew on the trees along the banks, making natural swings for the boys to fly out over the stream and drop into the water. He fished in the Walnut and the many creeks that fed into it and he picked berries, pawpaws, and sand plums. In the fall he gathered nuts that grew on the walnut trees that covered much of the uncleared land along the river that got its name from the trees. His father kept a horse and young Will White and the other boys played in the barn loft, where they had rigged up a trapeze and a turning bar.

51

White, slender and agile, could run like a deer and he was especially adept at turning cartwheels and handsprings and standing on his head.

But along with all the things that all boys did, he had read and read and, when he was graduated from the El Dorado High School in 1884, he was eager to attend college. From the time he was a small boy he loved music and when he was still in the grades he could play by ear on the organ or piano the popular tunes of the day as well as the old favorites in the hymnbooks. As he heard a new tune, he would learn to whistle it and then it was only a matter of getting to an organ or piano before he could make a fair presentation of it. At the town dances, where the young people gathered, at the parties in the homes of his friends, and at country dances, his interest was more in the music than in the dancing and it was not long until he not only was playing the piano, but he also was "calling" them. He could "follow" any tune the fiddlers played and he loved it.

Recently when Emporia had a formal opening for its new $600,000 Civic Auditorium, the last night's event was a grand ball. Mr. White, who had worked for such a building, in which the town could have trade shows, agricultural displays, public meetings, shows, and dances, attended all five of the night attractions. In his paper he had for years urged the construction of such a community center and now that it was here, he was ready to enjoy it with the rest of the community. While he and Mrs. White did not dance, they sat for three and a half hours along the side lines with hundreds of other spectators and watched the dancing to Duke Ellington's Negro swing band, to which the Chamber of Commerce paid $1,100. While it was a far cry from the dances he had attended and played for as a boy, this modern party recalled to Mr. White his days as an active musician, and the morning after the big ball he sat down and dictated an editorial.

"And now about the music," he wrote, after telling about the crowd. "But before we go into that, as the lawyers say, let us qualify as an expert. Fifty-five years ago and more the writer hereof earned his first dollar playing for dances in Butler County, a young boy in his middle teens. We made no boasts but our outfit, consisting of a blind fiddler, a competent cornetist, and deponent at the cabinet organ or piano, as the case happened to be, used to go out into the country to farm dances, where they took down the bed and the cookstove and emptied the houses and danced in three rooms. Mostly we played square dances, though we

53

had two or three waltzes—'The First Kiss Waltz,' 'The Cornflower Waltz,' 'The Skaters,' 'Where, Oh, Where Has My Little Dog Gone?' There wasn't a note in the lot. We all played by ear. As for calling off the square dances, the blind fiddler couldn't see to do it, the cornetist was busy with something else, so it fell upon this affiant to play the cabinet organ and call off—by which task we had to let out a boy's changing voice so that, after a year of it, we could be heard on a clear, windless, moonlit night in three townships, and we made a hogcaller look like a Quaker meeting. We were, in a way, the white Duke Ellington of the Walnut Valley. So, looking back over nearly sixty years, we can persuade the gentle reader that we know something about dance music as the light fantastic—or more or less fantastic—Kansas toe was tripped in the middle or early 1880's."

In describing the Ellington music, which he said "squawked and shrieked and roared and bellowed in syncopated savagery," Mr. White concluded with: "If that noise last night in the Civic Auditorium, for which the town paid $1,100 to Mr. Duke Ellington, is music, then the subscriber hereto is a trapeze performer."

And by that the people of Emporia knew exactly

what the editor of the *Gazette* thought about modern
swing music, for now he is short, fat, and easily winded
and no one would think that sixty years ago he was a
trapeze performer in his barn-loft gym.

Despite his great desire to read, Mr. White was not
a remarkable student in college, and, while students
at the College of Emporia today are reminded frequently that Mr. White once attended there, his scho-
lastic record is never mentioned and it is something he
does not brag about. But after his freshman year in
college in Emporia, which he left to go back to El
Dorado to help his mother and learn the printer's
trade, the young man began to realize that he needed
further education and his mother agreed. The printing part of the newspaper had not exactly appealed to
him and he had had a taste of the writing end which,
he said, looked like more fun and also offered greater
opportunities. Both he and his mother agreed that, if
he was going to write, he should have more education
and in 1886 he enrolled at Kansas University at Lawrence. He attended four years and I know of no other
four years in his life of which he has spoken less. He
never leads one to believe he was graduated from the
university, although he often has said he wished he
had completed the work for a diploma. But at the uni-

versity, as during his first year in the little Presbyterian college in Emporia, he found so many other things to interest him that he neglected his lessons. He continued to read everything in sight and he went through the school library from one end to the other, reading all the books, magazines, and newspapers that interested him. He continued his music and played with the school orchestra.

"I played with it until they found out how good I was," he said. "Everything was running smoothly until one time they put a piece of music in front of me and it was something I had never heard. The others went through it and I sat there and couldn't play a note. They hadn't noticed until then that I had been playing strictly by ear, but it didn't take them long to decide they needed a new piano player."

Part of the time during his four years at Kansas University, White worked for a Lawrence newspaper as a reporter, but the things he wrote apparently did not attract much more attention than did his scholarship record. Seldom is Mr. White's newspaper work in Lawrence recalled today, and when it is, it usually is the story he wrote of a wedding.

"It was a pretty good society item," he relates, "even if I do say so myself. I told all about the wedding and what the bride wore, but at the end I wrote: 'The happy couple will continue to live at No. —— on —— Street.' That was a mistake that kept me off the main street and running up and down the alleys for weeks trying to gather news. That 'happy' couple would have killed me if they had ever caught me."

In an Emporia café recently, when Mr. and Mrs. White happened to be eating luncheon downtown because their housekeeper was not well and they had invited three or four of the men from the office to eat with them, Mr. White saw a young man from out of town, whose father the editor had known at the university. For a moment he became reminiscent of his college days in Lawrence.

"I didn't learn a lot at school, but I did learn one thing," he said. "I knew when they had done all they could for me with what they had to work with. Some of the boys went five years and some of them six trying to get their diplomas. I had sense enough to know after four years that I was through and I got out."

Quitting school for good in 1890, Mr. White returned to El Dorado and this time he did not go to the *Weekly Democrat* office, but he got a job as a printer on the *El Dorado Republican*. Within a year he served as circulation manager, reporter, advertising solicitor, and then manager, hiring and firing the men, getting out the local items, and writing the editorials while his employer was in the state senate being a statesman. White was paid $18 a month as a printer when he started, and after becoming manager he received such little more pay that he quit his job and went to Kansas City. He became an editorial writer for the old *Kansas City Journal* and shortly afterward was sent to Topeka, the capital of Kansas, as the *Journal's* correspondent. Through friends of his father's and friends he had made working in El Dorado, the young correspondent knew many of the influential men in the Kansas statehouse and others who made politics more or less their business. Through these friends White was able to get many news stories which were off the beaten path and which other reporters and correspondents did not get. Many times he got tips on important stories before the other reporters knew about them. But his office did not always believe his stories until general announcement had been made and then all papers got the news which White had sent to his office in advance. This he could not take and he quit the *Journal,* but he went almost immediately to the *Kansas City Star,* where he was made an editorial writer.

Although he seldom talks of these early newspaper days when he worked for others, this period of Mr. White's life was not uneventful. He has written a little of the happenings and occasionally through the years, as something has happened to recall an incident of his life as a young reporter, he has told stories. Mostly they have been stories of troubles he had, similar to that of the write-up of the wedding in Lawrence.

"These pallid days upon which we have fallen do not recall the blithe gay years when reporting was combined with foot racing, mayhem, ground and lofty tumbling, buck and wing dancing, and assault with intent to kill," Mr. White wrote in 1917, when Colonel J. E. House, in an editorial in the *Topeka Capital,* became philosophical and called upon the editor of *The Emporia Gazette* to write the story of the lady who chased him with a buggy whip. Mr. White replied that House's suggestion was not a bad one, but that he was saving the story for a plan he had "been maturing for years" to write his recollections of the old days of the Kansas press and of his own life. That was in 1917. Today, more than twenty-three years later, the plan is still maturing, apparently, for the story has not yet appeared. Mr. White did, however, oblige Colonel House to some extent, for he wrote sketchily of a lot of episodes that occurred during his reporting days in El Dorado, Lawrence, and Kansas City.

Many times I have tried to draw these stories out of him in more detail, but hardly does he get started when he sees something or thinks of something that makes him finish his story quickly and start a new conversation about some subject of current importance.

Rarely does Mr. White "spin yarns" of the older days as many persons his age do. He is too busy with things that are happening today or those that might happen tomorrow to dwell much upon the past. For that reason I doubt if ever he will write the story of his life. Mrs. White could write a beautiful story of her husband's career, but she, too, is so busy working with the present that she has little time for even thinking of other days, let alone writing of them.

Summing a dozen thrilling incidents into a few short paragraphs, Mr. White did, in answer to Colonel House's challenge in 1917, tell in an editorial something of the fast-and-furious life he led as a reporter.

"Thirty-two years ago this summer," he wrote, "we began to kick the heavy Colt's universal jobber (operate a job printing press), rustle personal news items

at the trains, and drop watermelon rinds on prominent citizens passing below as we molded public
opinion in the forms, hot and often rebellious, for the
columns of the *Butler County Democrat.* Our first
essay at reform was upon a gambler who had a little
stud game four doors down the hallway from the office
and who used to like to take out a girl we fancied in
a red-wheeled buggy. That red-wheeled buggy gave
us a realizing sense of the wickedness of the gambler's
life. So, while the editor was out of town, we slipped
an item into the paper about the stud game which
the city marshal could not well overlook. The item
was a mistake. That gambler sat up out of hours four
long days trying to get a chance to kick our base of
supplies into our subconsciousness and only a fleet
and earnest pair of young feet kept the gambler from
achieving his end. Incidentally, he got the girl. Which
taught us a lesson about the gratitude of republics.

"The year following, while riding the hook-and-
ladder truck to fires and drawing $8 a week on the
El Dorado Republican, we were persuaded by a local
advertiser to make a few sensible remarks about a lady
peddling corsets in the town, who was taking business
from the merchant prince. The lady went into the
harness shop, bought a keen rawhide, and walked

61

Main Street and Sixth Avenue for two days and haunted the *El Dorado Republican* office at all hours for the reporter. The boss and the foreman expressed virtuous indignation at the reporter, and he made his beat from the alleys, meekly peering into a store from the back room to see if she was there before entering it, and never getting far from the alley door. We wrote our copy on the back stairs and sent it in by the devil, who once, being eager for a foot race or Something Equally Good, told the waiting and obdurate woman where we were perched. Then that episode passed, and we roasted a circus that didn't advertise enough to suit our nice taste in those matters, and if the circus had sent a sober man to do its fighting, he might have caught us.

"In those El Dorado years we attempted to paralyze the Farmers' Alliance, and were ridden in effigy through the streets of the town; a boycott was declared on the paper, and the candidate for county attorney on the Alliance ticket bought a gun to answer our charges.

"Then we moved to Lawrence, where we have winged many a gay mile down Massachusetts Street before irate citizens and have faced many a furious mob of Democrats in the office, coming in to stop subscriptions and order out advertising. Once Jerry Glad-heart—peace to his ashes—sent word that he would shoot us on sight, and once Pete Foley came in to call with a large, feverish ball bat, and remained to pray. Life at Lawrence was just one long, gorgeous flirta-tion with violent death. The only flash of light that illumines those Lawrence literary days in our memory was the friendship of Nash Walker, a colored porter in the Eldridge House, who afterwards became famous as an actor and once, in New York, let us touch the hem of his fame and stand in the reflected glory of our association. Nash never tried to kill us. But he sat on the reporter's desk and grinned that incandescent smile of his while a drunken printer with a long-bladed knife came in one midnight and chased us all over the room, out into the business office, and through the stock room. Nash certainly had a sense of humor, and the thought of a printer killing us who had no special grievance other than that we had asked him for a quarter he had borrowed, while good and vir-tuous burglars whom we had libeled and slandered had failed to wing us—the subtle humor of that situa-tion certainly did give Nash a few merry moments.

"In Kansas City life grew gradually dull and mo-notonous. A glance into the howitzer carried by Joe

Davenport, who came to whip the editor of the *Star*, and a leap from the second story of the building to a desk in the business office of the *Star* on the first floor, to escape the gun, was the most considerable episode that came to relieve the drab life. A delegation from the stockyards once came to fight, but we were out and they ignobly let the matter drop. A leading citizen named Owsley and a gentleman named Blitz obligingly threatened to kill us, but without lasting and satisfactory results. So we left Kansas City for Emporia, where for a few years business did pick up. We were slugged by a prominent citizen, chased by a lady, laid for by a female jointist with a pistol, and hanged in effigy in a Populist parade. A Negro murderer once tried to fuss his way into fame through our remains, which would not remain remains, and a local statesman once removed a big gun from an indignant reader of the *Gazette* who desired our blood. The committee has told us we had to leave town, bankers have warned us against our past-due paper, and once our dog was poisoned by designing enemies."

The *Gazette* Was Started in a Small Room on the Second Floor of This Building, but It Had Moved When Mr. White Bought the Paper in 1895. This Building Was Razed in the Building Boom of the Twenties.

CHAPTER VII

MARRIED—AND BROKE!

WHILE WORKING FOR THE *STAR* IN Kansas City, Mo., Mr. White met Miss Sallie Lindsay, a Kansas City, Kans., schoolteacher, who was popular among the younger society sets on both sides of the Kaw River which separates the two Kansas Cities. Some of the young men working for the *Star*, including Mr. White, ran around with the society crowd, and White, who always seemed to have an eye for the ladies, decided this pretty young teacher was the one for him. In less than a year after they met, they were married, on Apr. 27, 1893.

The bridegroom apparently did not write the account of his wedding for his paper, for the *Star* on the day of the wedding referred to the bride as "Miss Sally (instead of Sallie) Lindsay . . . a widely known young society woman with a host of friends."

Marrying Sallie Lindsay probably was the most important thing Mr. White ever did in his life. Another woman might have made a satisfactory wife for him, but those who have known them long agree that never were two people more suited for each other. I have stayed with them in their home and at the summer cottage in Colorado, I have been on long trips with them, and I have been with them through joyous and sad occasions, and never have I seen either let the other down. They have been fifty-fifty partners in everything and Mr. White has never made a major decision at the office or at home without first consulting Mrs. White. And she is his best critic—no little "yes woman," but one who tells him firmly if she believes he is making a mistake. They must have had quarrels during their forty-seven years of married life, for they are human and no human is perfect, but whatever family disagreements they might have had have been settled so quickly or kept so privately that no one outside of the family has heard of one.

A honeymoon is always an adventure, but when Mr. and Mrs. William Allen White left Kansas City on Apr. 27, 1893, for a three weeks' wedding trip, they probably would have been frightened to death had they known how it was going to end. Passing through Emporia on the train, they were met by friends Mr. White had made in his first year of school and later in his political reporting in Topeka. Then they sped on westward, going first to Montezuma, the hot springs near Las Vegas, N. M., where they spent nearly two weeks. Then they went to Santa Fe, before turning back toward Colorado, where they spent a few days at Manitou. Leaving their money in a bank in Manitou, on which they could write checks, they went to Estes Park, near Denver, for the last few days of the wedding trip. And in those last few days came the crash of the panic of 1893 and all their money, except a few dollars they had in their pockets, was lost when the bank at Manitou went busted.

Hardly had they heard the news of the bank's closing when a worse blow was struck. The *Star,* retrenching during the panic, telegraphed Mr. White that he no longer had a job.

"We were two of the sickest looking newlyweds you ever saw," says Mr. White now, "but before we could decide what to do we got another telegram from the *Star.* One of the older editorial writers was stricken with a heart attack and the *Star* not only wired me to come back but sent money for me to travel on. I had only enough for one ticket, so I left Mrs. White out there until I could send for her and I hurried back to work before they changed their mind again."

Later the other editorial writer regained his health, but the *Star* still kept White.

His childhood in El Dorado, his school days in Emporia and Lawrence, and his newspaper days in El Dorado and Lawrence held much for the young man from Kansas. Life in Kansas City, Mo., even though it was not a large city as large cities go, did not appeal to Mr. White. While he enjoyed editorial writing because he could write what he thought—even though the editor of the *Star* did not always print it—Mr. White missed the contact with the people that he had had in the country towns of Kansas. He liked a town where he could cover the entire business district on foot and still be within a few minutes' walk of the office. And like most young newspapermen then and now, he longed for a paper of his own.

Emporia, his birthplace, had always appealed to Mr. White. The Presbyterian College of Emporia and the State Normal School, with their students and teachers, made Emporia the kind of a town he liked. Emporia had its business side, with its flour mills, iron foundry, division headquarters of the Santa Fe Railroad, and its farming territory, but it also had a cultural side which appealed. The colleges influenced the town, not just by bringing in gay young people to attend school, but the influence was felt socially and in entertainment. Stars of the concert hall and stage stopped to perform in Emporia, although they skipped many Kansas towns which were larger. With the diversified business and the aesthetic touch of the colleges, Emporia had everything, Mr. White decided, and for two years after his marriage he kept in touch with Emporia through his friends and through visits, always with the idea in his head that here was a town in which he would like to edit the leading newspaper.

Emporia had many newspapers during its early days—some went broke quickly, some flourished, and some were merged with larger papers owned by stronger editors. *The Emporia Gazette* had been founded in 1890 by J. R. Graham, who had been one of the owners of the *News,* which was consolidated with the *Republican* earlier that year. The first issue of the *Gazette* was printed in August of 1890 and on May 20, 1892, W. Y. Morgan, who moved to Emporia from Cottonwood Falls, bought it for $2,000. Morgan, after three years in Emporia, decided to cast his lot in a larger town which was growing faster than Emporia, and on June 1, 1895, he sold it to White.

The little daily, published in a one-room building on a side street a half block off Commercial Street, the main thoroughfare, had about $1,500 worth of equipment and printing material, but its business and good will were worth something and White, without any money of his own, paid $3,000 for the business. He borrowed $1,000 from Governor E. N. Morrill, $1,000 from the estate of Preston B. Plumb, one of the town's founders; $700 from Major Calvin Hood; and $300 from George Plumb, all secured by bankable notes. The Emporians loaned the money because they believed in the town and the paper and had faith in the young editor. Mr. White had been a correspondent in Topeka for a Kansas City paper during part of the term of Morrill as governor and this official had faith in White. This faith, backed by the securities which were as good as money at the bank, made it comparatively easy for White to raise the money.

He repaid the thousand dollars to the Plumb estate with the profits of his first book, "The Real Issue," published a year after he bought the *Gazette*. The Morrill and the Hood notes were paid after the publication of "The Court of Boyville." The $300 he borrowed from George Plumb was paid with *Gazette* earnings and most of it was cleaned up by 1900, when the *Gazette* moved from rented quarters on a side

street to its own building in its present location, next
door to the post office. Again Mr. White had gone
into debt, but that always has been his policy. "To
keep in debt serves as an incentive to keep at work,
to keep down my natural laziness," he has often said.

But it was not so easy as it sounds, this buying the
Gazette with $3,000 of borrowed money and paying it
all back in five years, and even on the day Mr. White
came to Emporia to take charge of the paper he had
a serious matter to consider.

Leaving Mrs. White with her family in Kansas City,
Mr. White came alone to Emporia to take charge of
the paper, coming on the Santa Fe and having in his
pocket, when he got off the train, only $1.25. Whether
to walk uptown and save a fifth of all the ready cash
he had in the world or whether to spend a quarter,
ride the hack, and arrive in style was his problem.
Telling himself that a newspaper was an important
part of a town and that its editor also must be important, he climbed aboard the hack and, feeling much
like a president on his way to the inauguration, the
editor-to-be rode in style to the town's best hotel.

He lived on the money which came to the paper
from advertising and subscriptions and he watched his
accounts closely. He met the pay roll that first Satur-

71

day—as he has every week since he has been here—
but on the Monday after the first Saturday he had to
go to his men and borrow back some of the money to
pay for supplies to keep the paper going. But by
watching his collections with the same care he used
in making expenditures, he weathered the first few
weeks, and soon Mrs. White came to Emporia. In a
rented house they began housekeeping, and the young
editor and his wife felt they were firmly established.

During all the years he had worked on other papers,
Mr. White had dreamed of the day when he would
own his own, and he long before had decided how he
felt a newspaper should be operated and the place
an editor should hold in relation to the community.
The responsibility he felt was not kept a secret, and,
three days after taking over the *Gazette,* his position
was made clear in an editorial, entitled "Entirely
Personal."

"To the gentle reader who may, through the coming
years during which we are spared to one another, follow the course of this paper, a word of personal address
from the new editor of the *Gazette* is due," he wrote.
"In the first place, the new editor hopes to live here
until he is the old editor, until some of the visions
which rise before him as he dreams shall have come

true. He hopes always to sign 'from Emporia' after his name when he is abroad, and he trusts that he may so endear himself to the people that they will be as proud of the first words of the signature as he is of the last words. He expects to perform all of the kind offices of a country editor in this community for a generation to come. It is likely that he will write the wedding notices of the boys and girls in the schools; that he will announce the birth of the children who will some day honor Emporia; and that he will say the final words over those of middle age who read these lines. His relations with the people of this town are to be close and personal. He hopes that they may be kindly and just. The new editor of the *Gazette* is a young man now, full of high purposes and high ideals. But he needs the close touch of other hands. His endeavor will be to make a paper for the best people of the city. But to do that he must have their help. They must counsel with him, be his friends, often show him what their sentiment is. On them rests the responsibility somewhat. The 'other fellows' will be around. They will give advice. They will attempt to show what the public sentiment is. They will try to work their schemes, which might dishonor the town. If the best people stay away from the editor's office, if they neglect

73

to stand by the editor, they must not blame him for his mistakes. An editor is not all wise. He judges only by what he sees and hears. Public sentiment is only the sentiment that prevails. Good sentiment, so long as it does not assert itself, so long as it is a silent majority, is only private sentiment. If the good, honest, upright, God-fearing, law-abiding people of any community desire to be reflected to the world, they must see that their private opinion is public opinion. They must stand by the editors who believe as they do.

"It is a plain business proposition. The new editor of the *Gazette* desires to make a clean, honest, local paper. He is a Republican and will support Republican nominees first, last, and all the time. There will be no bolting, no sulking, no 'holier than thou' business about his politics—but politics is so little. Not one man in ten cares for politics more than two weeks in the year. In this paper, while the politics will be straight, it will not be obtrusive. It will be confined to the editorial page, where the gentle reader may venture at his peril. The main thing is to have this paper represent the average thought of the best people of Emporia and Lyon County in all their varied interests. The editor will do his best. He has no axes to grind. He is not running his paper for a political pull. If he could get an office he wouldn't have it. He is in the newspaper business as he would be in the dry goods business—to make an honest living and to leave an honest name behind. If the good people care for a fair, honest, home paper, that will stand for the best that is in the town—here it is.

"In the meantime I shall hustle advertising, job work, and subscriptions, and write editorials and 'telegraph' twelve hours a day in spite of my ideals. The path of glory is barred hog tight for the man who does not labor while he waits.

"W. A. WHITE."

CHAPTER VIII

A PAPER'S CHARACTER DEVELOPS

GENERALLY SPEAKING, MR. WHITE HAS lived up to the policy he outlined in his first editorial. He has no desire ever to leave Emporia for more than a visit and even then he is anxious to get back after he has been gone only a few days. If he is close enough to telephone when he is away, he calls the office every day, even if he is gone for only a day. If he believes a telephone call is too expensive, he telegraphs. But he never is too far away to write regularly. The *Gazette* follows him, by fastest mail, wherever he goes, and I believe he reads it more closely when he is in New York than when he is in Emporia, for I have received many letters calling my attention to things in the paper which I think he might have overlooked had he been here.

"Someone used the word 'plaintiff' the other day in a court item," he wrote me from New York on Oct. 25, 1934. "I had to use the forceps to get the words 'defendant' and 'plaintiff' out of Gene (a former court reporter). Please take a lead column rule and gouge them with a Caesarian operation out of the man that wrote the Monday night's item about the Finney case."

I still have the note, written in longhand. Apparently he was reading the paper, saw the word "plaintiff," grabbed his big red pen and a note card from the desk of the National Arts Club, where he was staying, and wrote the message while he remembered it. The next day he dictated a letter to a stenographer, telling me what a fine paper we were getting out. Whenever Mr. White finds fault with an employee or his work, he is quick to find some word of praise for the same man.

It is not that the editor does not like to read the paper when he is at home, for he reads it every day, although seldom does he read all of it. He has trained the men in the office to tell him what is going on and by press time he always knows all the major happenings. But away from home, I have seen him many times grab the *Gazette* out of the mail and read all the local news at one sitting.

From time to time, as conditions arose, Mr. White has found it necessary to enlarge upon the policy of the paper, but he still sticks closely to his original premise. In 1903, eight years after he bought the paper, he wrote an editorial, "A Newspaper's Duty," which still is law around the *Gazette* office. Although most of the men now working in the editorial room have not read the editorial, they know the rules because they have heard them preached not only by the editor but by all the men who have been in the office long. This "editorial law" was written so that the town might know what to expect of the *Gazette* during an impending lawsuit involving some prominent Emporians.

"The only excuse an editor has for being is that his paper shall print the news," the editorial read. "The question that comes to every man running a newspaper is: What is news? That he must settle for himself, and, having found a rule, must stick as closely to it as possible. When an editor begins monkeying with his conscience, stretching his rule to shield his friends or to punish his enemies, he is lost. He becomes wobbly and has no anchor and no direction.

"Every day matters come up in every community, big or little, that are disagreeable to print. Nasty stories are always afloat. Gossip is always in the air. An editor in a town of one hundred people could fill a six-column daily every night with gossip alone, if he could keep from being lynched. Much of it would be false and all of it would be unfair. And yet often these matters come up in such a shape that they may not be ignored. And here is where an editor has to set his jaw and go ahead following his conscience without fear or favor. Such times come to every attorney, to every doctor, to every preacher, to every man in every relation of life. It is a safe rule to follow, that gossip may be ignored, no matter how loudly it buzzes, till it becomes a matter of court record. Then it may not be left out of the paper. If a man has a grievance against his fellow man that he or she is too cowardly to air in public court, it is safe to say that there are two sides to the question and the editor who prints the story prints it at his own peril. But on the other hand, when a man takes his grievance into court, when he spreads it upon the record and gives his opponent a chance to answer in an open, public manner, then the quarrel, no matter whom it involves, is a matter that no editor can overlook. And after a case gets into court, a newspaper should let the courts try it, printing the claims of each side, not trying to convict or acquit either of the parties.

"That, it seems to the *Gazette,* is the fair way to treat unsavory matters. No honest editor cares to have scandal and improper stories in his paper, and no one should print such stories in such a way that they may not be read aloud in the family circle. It is the way news is handled that counts for or against decency. A vile story may be handled with care and the readers be no worse for seeing it."

This principle has been followed in the *Gazette* office all during Mr. White's ownership. Naturally it has been necessary, to carry out this policy, to adopt some general rules, many of which are peculiar to Mr. White's paper. Among them is the divorce rule, to which the *Gazette* has adhered religiously.

"A divorce means the breaking up of a home and it is a sad affair, no matter how just it might be," Mr. White told me when I was a young courthouse reporter and came in with what I thought was a good story, listing all the reasons a woman had given for suing her husband. "Divorce doesn't affect only the man and the woman, but often there are children—innocent victims—and it means the breaking up of a home. Frequently a divorce suit is filed and later dismissed and a happy home is maintained. So remember that the filing of a divorce is not news unless it is incidental to some other happening which is news."

So the *Gazette* has a rule against printing news of

"Must have been about 1911 because I still had hair," Mr. White said. "That's about the last time I remember of having enough hair to really count."

the filing of divorce suits. An exception is the case of a prominent man, convicted of embezzlement, which was unknown to his wife before his arrest. The news of the embezzlement was of general interest and the court dockets were watched carefully, for, if this woman had sought divorce, that would have been news.

The *Gazette* does print the news of divorces being granted, but it always is a short statement of facts, telling who received the divorce and the custody of the children, if any, and the story always is on an inside page with a small headline. The reason for never leaving out news of a divorce granted, Mr. White explains, is because a divorce changes the legal status of two persons and the public has a right to know about it. The same thing is done in the case of a person adjudged insane or feeble-minded, although it is often difficult to hold to the rule when weeping relatives are in the office, begging that you leave the news out.

Mr. White has other rules, not common in most newspaper offices, which are more or less flexible but at the same time hold to a pattern and often make decisions border on the hairline. Generally a person not of legal age, or under twenty-one, is protected when he gets into trouble. The news of the trouble is

81

printed, but the name of the person involved is left out and no clue is given to his identity. Of course this is not true in major crimes, involving death or serious injuries. But for ordinary robberies, bad check cases, drunkenness, and the general run of crimes, minors are protected because, as Mr. White explains it, "a juvenile can make a lot of mistakes and still settle down and become a good citizen. But if he is branded publicly, his chances of reforming are hampered by the attitude of the people toward him."

First offenders in minor crimes, no matter what their age, also find a soft spot in Mr. White's attitude. If the person involved or a member of his family comes to the *Gazette* office to ask that the person's name be withheld, the request usually is granted. Believing that an ordinary traffic violation is not a crime and does not brand one as a criminal, Mr. White's code calls for the printing of names of all motorists convicted on driving charges. Mrs. White's name has appeared frequently in police news for violating parking regulations.

Drunken drivers are a problem in Kansas, where being drunk is a minor offense, driving while drunk is serious, and being caught in possession of any liquor containing more than 3.2 per cent alcohol means a minimum of thirty days in jail, a fine of $100, or both. Because the penalty for possessing liquor is so severe and that of being drunk is a minor offense, if a man is arrested and prosecuted at all, the tendency of too many Kansans when they have any liquor is to drink it as quickly as possible. And then many of the drunks get into cars. These men, who endanger the lives of others, find no sympathy in the *Gazette's* policy and any man convicted of driving while drunk gets the works as far as publicity is concerned.

"The penalty of the courts frequently doesn't bother the drunken drivers as much as does the publicity, so it seems to me our duty to make the highways and streets safer is to print the names of all drunken drivers," Mr. White explains periodically in editorials which serve as warnings to those who might get a snootful and get into a car. "A drunk at the wheel of a car is as dangerous as a drunk brandishing a gun and, while I feel sorry because he hasn't any better judgment, the drunken driver gets no consideration here," I heard Mr. White tell a young man, who long had been a friend of the paper, when he came over to ask that his name be left out of the paper. Even the old stories that "It will kill my poor, old, sick mother if she reads this in the paper" or "Think of the embarrassment it will cause my children at school" have no effect on the drunken driving regulation. Motorists or pedestrians who might be killed or injured by drunken drivers also have "poor, old, sick mothers" and children in school, and they deserve protection, the Emporia editor believes.

Competition has never been a serious worry to Mr. White, who believes that if an editor prints the best family newspaper in a town the people will read it and the advertisers will support it. Emporia long has had a weekly newspaper—a strictly Democratic paper—as opposition, but the Republican *Gazette* and the weekly are friendly competitors and are the best of friends. A dozen or more papers have been started in opposition to the *Gazette* but they have been short-lived and not because of any attack by Mr. White and his paper. Although some of them from the first have bitterly opposed the *Gazette* and its editor and have tried to pick fights in the public print, the *Gazette* has printed a news item about the new paper when it started and then ignored it.

"We'll spend our time trying to make our paper better and we'll continue to ignore what they say about us," the boss explained at an office conference a few years ago, when a man from a near-by town came

84

in with modern machinery, a chip on his shoulder, and plenty of plans for a new daily paper in Emporia. "You in the advertising department will continue to sell our paper on its merits without discussing the new paper and you in the editorial end just continue to make a good paper that people will want to read."

Two months later trucks drove up and carted the equipment of the new paper to another place.

In September, 1920, a few days after I came to work on the *Gazette* as a college student and reporter, the paper installed a new linotype—its fourth—and in an editorial announcing the improvement, Mr. White wrote:

"Fourteen men have come joyously into Emporia to fill a long-felt want with another paper—'a bright, snappy paper that would print all the news'—in the twenty-five years, and they have walked sadly out or have ridden to Maplewood cemetery."

CHAPTER IX

THE BOSS HIRES A NEW BOY

I FIRST MET WILLIAM ALLEN WHITE IN early September of 1920, the day I enrolled as a freshman at the College of Emporia, where he had entered as a freshman just thirty-six years before. Having worked as an electrician's helper, starting in the grade school and becoming a full-fledged electrician before graduation from high school, I had not thought of attending college, but a high school English teacher, Miss Pauline Sleeth, insisted that I should. I had stepped into a fair job with an electric company immediately after graduation and was content to stay there. But all summer long Miss Sleeth insisted that I go to the College of Emporia in the fall and get a job with Mr. White's *Gazette*. I had taken high school journalism under Miss Sleeth my senior year, merely because it looked like the easiest subject to fill out my graduation schedule. I had no particular interest in newspaper work, I was not the least bit interested in politics, economics interested me only to the extent of whether I had a decent job, and William Allen White was just another guy who owned a newspaper, as far as I was concerned. I was perfectly happy in another town 125 miles from Emporia, except that the teacher would not leave me alone and insisted I go to Emporia. Finally, just before school opened in the fall, I decided it would be easier to attend college one semester and then quit than to argue any longer with Miss Sleeth. To do that, I had to have a job while attending school and, again at Miss Sleeth's insistence, I promised to see Mr. White before trying an electric company. She had met him some years before when she taught in Cottonwood Falls, twenty miles from Emporia, and he was one of her idols. I was so little interested I did not even take the trouble to look him up in "Who's Who."

Arriving in Emporia early in the morning, I walked past the *Gazette* office several times, afraid to enter. An electric shop two doors from the *Gazette* and another in the next block had more attraction and it was a temptation to ask for a regular job and forget about school and the *Gazette,* but I remembered Miss Sleeth. Finally I decided I would enroll in college first and pay my tuition. Then I would have to get a job. So I

87

boarded one of the old electric streetcars—Emporia
had three in 1920—and rode out to the College of Emporia. By chance I was assigned a faculty adviser who
taught the school's two journalism classes. I told him
I was undecided as to a course of study but hoped to
get a job with the *Gazette* and before I hardly knew
what had happened, I had signed up for a course in
English, journalism, and a few incidental subjects and
had paid $48.50 of my only $75. Given a list of room-
ing houses at the college, I soon found a room and
paid a month's rent in advance, leaving me only
$14.50. That meant I had to get a job and undoubt-
edly I would have headed for one of the electric shops,
despite all of my good intentions, had not the journalism teacher told me that I probably would not be able
to land a job on the *Gazette* right away, but that I
might after I had completed my journalism course. I
had not been favorably impressed with the teacher in
the first place, probably because of the rapidity with
which he had signed me up. His belief that I could not
get on the *Gazette* made me determined that I would
get a newspaper job. But determination began slip-
ping when I walked into the front of the *Gazette* office
a little after five o'clock in the evening. Although the
door was unlocked, the front office was dark and no

one was in sight. The door of a big iron safe at the rear wall facing the door was closed and I hoped that the whole office was closed and no one was there. Wandering down a hall I came to another office with three desks, a couple of typewriters, and on the wall a big red sign with gold letters reading: "Cheer Up, There Ain't No Other Hell." I read the sign twice before I saw the little, fat, bald man scribbling at a desk almost under the sign. He went right on scribbling, seemingly unaware that I was standing and watching, and I was nearly ready to run out when he dropped a fat red fountain pen on the desk, looked up, and said impatiently: "Everybody else is gone. Is there anything I can do for you?"

"I guess not," I said, relieved both because someone had said something and because it had begun to look as if I could retreat. "I was just looking for Mr. William Allen White."

"Well," exclaimed the fat man at the desk, "if that's all you want, that's easy. I'm W. A. White."

I'll never know what I said after that except that I mumbled something about wanting a job and that a high school teacher had sent me. I must have told my name and that I had enrolled at the College of Emporia, for in what seemed like seconds I was dismissed with instructions to "come back tomorrow after school and maybe we can find a place for you."

Early the next afternoon, inquiring for Mr. White at the business office, I was waved to a little front office across the narrow hall from the business office which I had not even seen the night before. The floor was littered with newspapers, a big fireplace was filled with newspapers and wrapping papers, books were piled about on the floor, and Mr. White was sitting at the most littered desk I had ever seen. A cleared place in the middle was big enough only for the sheet of paper on which he was writing with his big red pen. Before I could speak he was on his feet and leading me to another office, where he left me standing beside a desk occupied by a young man who was marking up type-written pages.

"Cal, here's a boy who's going to the College of Emporia and needs a job," said Mr. White. "I told him we would give him a chance. Give him a ticket to the show up at the Normal School tonight, have him write us a funny piece about it, and bring it in tomorrow."

With that he went back into his office and left me standing there, a befuddled college freshman. After a few questions from "Cal," who I later learned was Calvin Lambert, the city editor, I was given a ticket and told to attend a stage show, "Twin Beds," in the State Teachers College auditorium that night and to have a piece about it in the office by eight o'clock the next morning.

"After that," said Lambert, "we'll have a place for you some place—if something doesn't happen."

I stopped in the front office again to thank Mr. White, who grinned and waved me away, but I was there long enough to hear Mr. Lambert in the next office say to someone: "My God! The boss has hired another damn kid who doesn't know anything."

That night I went to the show and it was hilariously funny, but I worried so much, knowing that I had to write something about it, it seemed like a tragedy. At the end of the first act a tall, young man I had seen in the *Gazette* office that afternoon came up and announced he was Eugene Lowther, a reporter. A few minutes later Mr. Lambert and his wife came along and they invited me to sit with them. After the show they took me to a downtown soda fountain for a drink and there I learned why I had been hired. My high school teacher had written Mr. White and told him she wanted me to have a job. She had sent my picture and some copies of some "Letters of a Freshman to His Folks in the Country" I had written for the high

91

school paper. Mr. White had lost track of both the picture and the letters, but he remembered the face and took a chance on giving me a job.

"It wouldn't have made any difference if there hadn't been any pictures or any letters," said Lambert. "He probably would have hired you. He hires anybody."

With that great send-off, I went home and tried to write a funny story about "Twin Beds." Because I thought the high school "freshman letters" might have impressed Mr. White, I wrote the story of the show in the form of a letter of a college freshman to his folks at home. Having a seven forty-five class in the morning, I left my story on Lambert's desk before anyone but the janitor had arrived and I went to school. That afternoon when I reported for work, Lambert took me into Mr. White's office and I was told that I was hired and that I was to write "Letters of a College Freshman" twice a week and to do anything else Lambert had for me to do.

Nothing was said about pay, either by Mr. White or Mr. Lambert, and things went like that for nearly two weeks. My mornings were spent in school and my afternoons walking up and down the main street, Commercial Street, gathering news items in the stores.

Copying news items sent in by the country correspondents and reading copy aloud to the proofreader while she corrected the proofs also were part of my job, which I had begun to like, except for the fact that I had spent all but a few cents of the money I had brought to Emporia. Finally I worked up enough nerve to ask Lambert when the *Gazette* had payday and he replied: "Why, last Saturday. Haven't you been paid? I thought Mr. White had taken care of that."

"Why, I thought you would fix that up," was Mr. White's answer when Lambert took me into the editor's office. After Mr. White had asked me how much I had to pay for room and meals and found out that I had to pay all my own expenses, he thought for a moment and asked: "Can you get along on twelve dollars a week? Of course you will be working only half a day and you are just beginning as a reporter, but it seems to me you ought to have that much to live on."

I would have taken the job for less for I knew I was not worth that much, but I did not object. Later I learned that another student reporter, who had begun nearly a year before I had, was making only eight dollars a week, but his parents lived in Emporia and he had no board and room to pay.

I tell all this not because my start as a *Gazette* employee was unusual, but because it is typical of the way the newspaper's forty employees began work there. *The Emporia Gazette* is unusual in that its employees seldom quit their jobs and the service records of the workers show that their terms of employment average far longer than those of employees on most newspapers. Of the forty employees now, one has been employed forty-one years, another forty, one thirty-five, one thirty-four, one thirty-three, and another twenty-six. The average length of service is seventeen and one-half years.

So many boys have begun work for Mr. White as I did, that some editors have dubbed the paper "The Gazette School of Journalism." And this "school" has been another of Mr. White's hobbies. Always he has loved young people and he has been happy when he could give them an opportunity to work even though they were without experience. When jobs got scarce after the crash of 1929, so many experienced newspapermen were available that young boys and girls just out of school and without experience could not get jobs. Editors of papers in larger cities long have told beginners seeking work that they should first get some experience in a small town, since the small towns were sending their experienced reporters to the city jobs and filling the ranks with beginners. But when jobs became scarce in the cities, the small-town reporters stayed at home and that left no place for the beginners to go. While the *Gazette* is only a country-town paper, it is widely known because of its editor and after the depression began the applications began pouring into the *Gazette* office faster than ever before. Boys and girls offered to work for any kind of wages on which they could exist, just to get started. Many offered to work for nothing, just for the experience and in hopes of a letter of recommendation from Mr. White and the *Gazette*.

The *Gazette* maintained its full force throughout the depression, although there were two wage cuts, so there were no jobs for beginners. But the applicants kept at it, not only writing, but coming to the *Gazette*. All of them, it seemed, wanted to be writers and no one wanted to solicit advertising. Mr. White worried about these youngsters who wanted experience and could not get it. Finally a boy who had been graduated from the University of Missouri journalism department was told he could work if he wanted to, but he would have to work regularly at all kinds of jobs and we could pay him nothing. He readily accepted and for three or four months he was on the job at eight o'clock every morning and he did not quit so long as there was anything to be done. He was given "mean" jobs, things the regular reporters did not like to do, such as copying long lists of names and copying country correspondence which was written in longhand, but he never shirked. Another boy who had been graduated from Emporia Teachers College came to the *Gazette* under the same conditions. A girl who had taught school in a village for a year and whose parents had moved to Emporia while she was teaching, decided she had had enough of teaching and she begged for an opportunity to get some experience. She was put to work on the same conditions.

Another youth, who had a good job in the circulation department of a large New York City daily, had always wanted a chance at news writing, but he had been discouraged in his own office. He saved his vacations for several summers and when he had six weeks coming to him, he got in his car and drove to Emporia. His grandmother, who lived in New York, was a friend of the Whites and through her he had heard of the *Gazette's* "school of journalism." He was put to work.

Another girl, whose home was a small Kansas town,

A Recent Picture of Mr. and Mrs. White.

was graduated from Wellesley College in Massachusetts and after a few months at home she came to Emporia for a job—a child full of enthusiasm and eager to work. She was given the opportunity.

One girl from Ohio, whose father was a schoolteacher, was sent through college on condition that she teach school at least three years before trying any other kind of work. She had longed for a job with a newspaper since she was in high school and, as soon as she finished her third year as a teacher, she went to Cincinnati and asked for a newspaper job. After an interview, the editor, impressed with her eagerness, told her that if she got some experience on a small-town paper and made good, he would give her a job later.

"What kind of a small-town paper?" asked the girl. "Which would be the best one?"

The editor suggested that she write to Mr. White in Emporia, but instead of writing she packed her belongings, jumped into her car, and drove to Emporia. No one here had ever seen or heard of her and Mr. White was busy in his private office when she arrived. She refused to talk with anyone else until Mrs. White came in. So impressed was Mrs. White that she invited the girl to the White home for dinner and to spend the night.

"We'll see about the job in the morning," I heard Mrs. White tell her as I left the office hurriedly, for I already had three such workers in our editorial department.

But the next morning Mr. White brought her in and told me her story briefly and left her there with the admonition:

"You do what you want to about her. You know better than I how many of these people you can stand without disrupting your staff and wearing yourself out, and I'm not asking you to take her."

I heard the girl's story and she started work.

In five or six years the *Gazette* must have had twenty-five or thirty such volunteer workers or, as we called them, "students in the W. A. White School of Journalism." About half of them made good. Some just did not have it in them to be reporters and others started out well but, apparently because they were not getting paid, they felt they had to do only those things they wanted to do. We weeded them out as quickly as possible when it appeared they were not happy or we were not satisfied. Usually we had only one at a time working on that basis, although several times there were two. For two months one summer there were six and Emporia never before or since has been combed so thoroughly for news. Naturally a paper as small as the *Gazette* could not print everything they brought in, so the competition was keen among the beginners to write things which would get in the paper and later bring them better assignments. Much of the time they were left to their own resources to dig up what they could, but even then they required supervision and someone had to look over what they had written. At the end of the summer I was a wreck and resolved that never again would we have more than one apprentice reporter at a time.

"I don't blame you," was Mr. White's answer when I told him. "If you hadn't made the decision, I was going to make it for you. As badly as we feel for these children who can't get jobs, we can't wreck ourselves."

But watching the way the novices turned out was somewhat of a reward and it is a nice feeling to know that a dozen or more of the boys and girls now have good jobs on newspapers. The word spread that the *Gazette* always had a surplus of reporters and frequently other editors wrote or telephoned when they needed someone. Knowing most of the editors and papers in this part of the country, it was not hard to

99

determine which one of our "students" might fill the bill. In several instances no one was recommended because we did not feel that we had anyone who would satisfy the particular editor who needed someone.

All this did not keep anyone from a regular job on the *Gazette*. The paid staff was maintained at its usual strength through it all and the regular workers fell into the scheme and helped the new ones. Some of this was because the extra workers made the chores of the regulars somewhat easier, but all over the *Gazette* office there was a general desire to help the beginners. Part of this could be attributed to the fact that most of the *Gazette* reporters had been, like myself, put to work when no one really was needed.

But the wage and hour law and minimum wage regulations stopped the *Gazette* journalism school. The beginners were not allowed to work without pay and we couldn't afford to pay them and maintain our regular staff. Letters of application still come in from all over the country—about a dozen a week—and the applicants continue to appear in person—willing to work for nothing. But nothing can be done about it. The "school" has closed.

100

CHAPTER X

THE GAZETTE FAMILY

M R. WHITE FREQUENTLY SPEAKS OF "the *Gazette* family" in referring to his employees, and it literally is a business family. Mr. White knows every employee intimately; he knows the wives of the married men and even away from the office on the street he recognizes the children of the employees. Mrs. White, who takes about as much interest in the affairs at the office as does the editor, can do better than he does in the matter of the families, for she can sit down and write the names of all the employees, she can check those who are married, and she can name practically all the employees' children. She proved this at the last Christmas dinner given by the Whites at a downtown hotel for all employees, wives, and children. Suffering from a cold, she was warned by her doctor to stay in for a few days, but she didn't let that stop her from planning the dinner. Sitting at home she made a chart of the hotel dining room, with its ten

101

large tables, and made the seating arrangements for everyone. Then she telephoned to the office and gave the plans to one of the women in the business office, who checked the lists and went to the hotel to arrange the place cards. Mrs. White had not left out a person. Then Mrs. White disobeyed the doctor's orders and attended the dinner.

Both Mr. and Mrs. White love children, and much is made over a birth in a *Gazette* family. The Whites take a financial as well as an affectionate interest in these babies and for nearly twenty-five years the hospital bills for births in families of all *Gazette* employees have been paid by the Whites. While this is one form of employee benefit the unmarried workers do not share in, I have heard complaints from the single employees in only one instance, and that was in the case of a man who already had so many children his weekly wage was barely enough to take care of the family expenses. But in this case the unmarried employees did no more talking than those who were married and had also shared in the "Whites' hospital fund." In fact it was a married man with a family who told a group gathered around a linotype one morning before work began: "A few people around here seem to have the idea that, because the Whites pay the hospital bills, they are making more money when they have babies."

"The *Gazette* family" is no different from regular families. There are those employees of the *Gazette* who do not particularly care for other employees; there are all kinds of petty jealousies and rivalries; and in some instances there are those who are not above thinking that some employee is "soldiering" on the job and stays on because he is a "pet" of Mr. White or a favorite of a department head or because Mr. White is particularly adverse to seeing anyone discharged. There probably is no employee who has not been criticized or even "cussed out" by some other worker, but the cases have been rare when any employee would let an outsider get away with any criticism of another *Gazette* employee. This trait undoubtedly is unconsciously adopted by the *Gazette* workers from Mr. White, who will listen eagerly to any fair complaint about one of his workmen but who also makes the complainant listen to his defense of the man.

Mr. White's supervision of his employees is done largely by suggestion. Rarely does he command someone to do or not to do something. Major changes in office organization or policy generally are decided

103

in conferences of department heads, frequently over the luncheon table. The conferences are held at luncheon because Mr. White likes to see his employees enjoy a good meal and partly because mealtime is one time of the day when he can sit down and do something without being interrupted. In the twenty years I have been with the *Gazette,* there has not been a major decision affecting more than one department of the paper or concerning the purchase and installation of a linotype, press, or any other large piece of machinery that has not been talked over at least once at a luncheon table by the department heads and some of the workers affected by the change.

Mrs. White, who in no way attempts to "run the office" or pry into its affairs, takes a great interest in all these major changes, especially in changes of personnel, and I have seen her sit for two hours in a conference, frequently offering helpful suggestions or criticisms of news or advertising policies. The *Gazette* probably would have had a photoengraving plant long ago had it not been for Mrs. White, who contends that a newspaper should concentrate on "word pictures" rather than photographs.

"Perhaps I'm old-fashioned," she has said many times, "but I still believe that a story well written—

briefly, entertainingly, and to the point—means a lot more to the reader than a photograph."

Mrs. White, who in recent years has written little for the *Gazette*, has not forgotten the earlier days when she helped Mr. White with the office work—when they first bought the paper and again later when many of the employees were in the army during the World War. She can still write a good news story, a timely editorial, or a pertinent book review. An example was her description of the sailing of the Whites' son, W. L. "Young Bill" White, when he left New York in October, 1939, to cover the European war news for a newspaper syndicate. This descriptive piece, in which she gave in detail the preparations Bill made for his stay in the war zone, was mailed back to the *Gazette* and was reprinted in papers all over the United States. She has done book reviews for the leading book pages and literary magazines. Although she writes much more slowly and deliberately than her famous husband, and her style is much simpler, she writes with force and frequently her pieces are credited to Mr. White.

Mrs. White is one of the best sources of news the *Gazette* reporters have, and whenever she hears anything that is news she calls the office. Hardly a morning passes but she telephones the society editor some

105

tips for social items, and more often than not Mrs. White will give the reporter a peculiar slant to a story which makes it more readable than the run-of-the-mill social notes.

The *Gazette* could not have too many short items about individuals to suit Mrs. White, and she continually points out that Emporia is a country town even if it has 14,000 people and a big trade territory and that the "locals" should not be neglected. Mr. White, too, calls for more personal items—two- and three-line pieces about Emporians going away, coming home, or having guests. But the men at the office disagree with the idea that there cannot be too many of them. While the *Gazette* is a country-town paper, Emporia is the shopping center of a territory within a radius of fifty miles of Emporia. The *Gazette* has hundreds of subscribers in the smaller towns in this territory and these people read the *Gazette* for its district news, its Associated Press reports, and its features rather than its strictly Emporia news. To maintain a balance of local news for the Emporians—and the Whites—and the district and world news and features for both the Emporians and the readers out in the territory is a difficult job.

"When it comes to those local items," I told Mr.

106

and Mrs. White once, when they said we needed more local items, "the *Gazette* is just like a boy who is too big for short pants and his parents don't think he is big enough for long ones."

"Go along with you," answered Mrs. White. "Tell your reporters we need some more local items and don't let your pants get too big for you."

To solve the problem, we have adopted a policy of using all the local items which are telephoned or brought to the office and of calling for personal items concerning the town's more prominent citizens. Apparently it has worked, for the *Gazette's* circulation has grown steadily in recent years.

Mr. White has done innumerable things for Emporia, not only by using his editorial and news columns to boost them, but by actually getting into the harness and working. A civic auditorium, convention hall, or exposition room for many years was one of his dreams and he worked hard to get such a building, but three times in the late nineteen twenties and early nineteen thirties such a building was voted down at the polls by the people. Emporia's $615,000 Civic Auditorium, which was completed in the spring of 1940, is a dream-come-true for the Emporia editor.

If you would walk out on Commercial Street today

and begin asking people who was responsible for the auditorium, those who remembered anything about it at all would tell you that the Citizens' Committee conceived the idea and conducted the successful campaign for a bond issue which was voted by the people. If you would ask the members of the Citizens' Committee, which finally had a membership of fifty or sixty men, who in the organization was responsible, you probably would be told half a dozen names, none of which would be right. Three or four might remember that it was Mr. White who started the Citizens' Committee and one or two might realize that Mr. White first suggested the auditorium as a project. But he did the whole thing with such subtlety that few, if any at all, knew what had happened after it was all over.

For a year or a year and a half Mr. White had a series of luncheons in a private dining room at the Broadview Hotel, inviting each time from a half dozen to a dozen men. They always were held on Saturday noon, but without any regularity, and he averaged about three or four every two months. One Saturday he would have a group of preachers and the next he might have bankers. Sometimes the groups were mixed, but during the series he invited and fed, in addition to the preachers and bankers, merchants of all

kinds, farmers, cattlemen, millers, lawyers, school officials, bakers, city and county officers, welfare workers,
motorcar dealers, utilities men, and even clerks and
bookkeepers who had shown an interest in civic affairs.

One or two men from the *Gazette* always attended
the meetings and I was at all of them, but never was
I told more than any of the other guests about what
was going on. I did not ask, for I thought that if the
boss had anything up his sleeve and wanted me to
know what it was, he would tell me. I decided that if
he did not have anything in particular in mind and
merely wanted to be a good host, I would be a good
guest and keep still. But always I looked for the "nig-
ger in the woodpile," yet today I still do not know if
there was one in this long series of luncheons.

At each luncheon the men would be served a good
meal, which had been ordered by Mr. White in advance. The usual sixty-cent luncheon featured by the
hotel was waived by the editor. Thick, rare steaks and
beef rib roasts with baked potatoes, topped off with
big slices of pie or baked apples, were served, the meals
always costing from seventy-five cents to a dollar. Mr.
White never ate what the others did but stuck to his
traditional noon diet of whole-wheat toast, in milk, a
pot of coffee, and a pitcher of hot milk with which

109

he mixed his own half-and-half drink, and a baked apple, fresh figs, or stewed prunes for dessert. Mr. White always liked to have the same waitress and he always gave her a generous tip, but he kept her busy heaping the platters of hot biscuits, filling gravy boats with honey, or seeing that the pitchers contained enough cream for all the men who wanted it on their baked apples. During the meal the talk would run as it would among any group of men eating together— just table talk. Then after everyone had said he had had enough to eat, Mr. White would jerk his napkin from the top of his vest, where he always tucks one corner if he remembers it, fold it carelessly, lean forward on the table, and announce:

"Well, I haven't anything in particular on my mind, but I thought maybe some of you might have. I've just been so busy putting out a paper (he would vary this with 'writing a book,' 'attending the national political conventions,' 'attending some meetings in the East,' or whatever he might have been doing) that I thought I might have lost out on what was going on around here. I haven't anything to tell you. I just wanted to see you and find out if everything was going all right."

Sometimes the men would remain for ten minutes

and sometimes for an hour, the conversation usually going from one thing to another with everyone having an opportunity to get across anything he wanted to say. Aside from the sociability, the meetings were profitable for the *Gazette*. Mr. White frequently came away with ideas for editorials and always there were tips for news stories.

One Saturday noon, arriving at the hotel with Mr. White, I was surprised to find he had invited about two dozen men and all from different businesses. Most of them, however, had been at one or more of the luncheons before. And after the meal, Mr. White sprung another surprise.

"I've been thinking," he told the group, "that we need a city auditorium or a community building or something of the kind. We need a place for conventions, trade shows, manufacturers' exhibits, merchants' expositions, farm and cattle shows, and exhibits for the things produced by the boys and girls in our 4-H Clubs. I know this thing has been up before and it has lost, but we still need it and I've just been wondering what we can do to help it along, who can start it, and why the other propositions were voted down."

All the men in this group were enthusiastic and in the conversation the men and groups who had opposed

111

the previous bond issues were named. It also was brought out that many voted against the civic building because they thought it was "something the Chamber of Commerce is trying to cram down our throats."

"Why doesn't some other organization sponsor it?" suggested Mr. White. "Some of you men don't belong to the Chamber of Commerce. Why don't you start a new organization? Some of you have business connections with or are friends of some of the men and organizations which have been against an auditorium. Why don't you get them interested? You don't have to mention the auditorium. A lot of working men in this town need jobs. Just get some of their leaders to talking about what would make jobs and some of them will suggest an auditorium. If they won't support it when we start it, why let's let them start it and we'll help them. We don't care who starts it, but Emporia needs a big building where we can have all these things that will bring in people from all over our territory as well as be a center of activity for Emporians."

The upshot of the meeting was that a group of men would meet soon to form a citizens' committee to discuss the needs of Emporia. Men who had opposed the community building would be expressly but tactfully invited not only to take part but to take leadership.

(*Photograph by Paul Chandler.*)

Emporia's New $600,000 Civic Auditorium.

(*Photograph by Paul Chandler.*)

As Travelers on U. S. Highway 50S See Emporia's Business District.

Shortly the group met, someone suggested an auditorium, and soon the organized campaign was on with men from all parts of town and all kinds of business working together. Some of those who always had been for the project served as the guiding hands, but all were encouraged to take part. Not only did Emporia vote for a $300,000 bond issue, but some new civic leaders were developed. After the bonds were voted, the Federal government again began making Public Works Administration grants and the Emporia project was presented and approved as a project to receive 45 per cent Federal aid. When a full block close to the business center of town was selected as a site, it developed that the city already owned some of the ground and the Federal government added to its quota 45 per cent of the land the city owned. The result was a huge brick and stone building with a main auditorium seating 4,500, a smaller auditorium for meetings of less than 400 persons, a full basement for trade shows and farm and manufacturers' expositions, and offices and quarters for all city departments, including a modern jail and fire department.

Long before the building was completed some of the men who had worked for it from the first wanted to name the structure "William Allen White Audito-

113

rium," but the boss said "No" loud and long, and I know he would not have stood for it even if the architect had not discovered that a building constructed with the help of Federal funds could not bear the name of an individual.

Never did Mr. White or the *Gazette* take any credit for the editor's part in getting the building for the town, and if this story reaches public print you will know that it got in without Mr. White's knowing of it. Many times since the auditorium has been in use it has been filled, but in the first eight months the attraction which filled it and then turned away the greatest number of persons was a free, public talk by W. L. White, son of William Allen White, soon after he returned to this country from touring Europe and reporting the Russian-Finnish war from the front lines for a newspaper syndicate and a broadcasting chain. And as Mr. and Mrs. William Allen White walked down the center aisle to their seats with other Emporians fifteen minutes before the speech started, the great crowd stood and cheered. Mr. White's heart was filled with pride that night, not only for his son but because Emporians had built such a big, beautiful and useful hall.

CHAPTER XI

A PARK FOR THE CHILDREN

PARKS LONG HAVE INTERESTED BOTH Mr. and Mrs. White, and the *Gazette* has continually worked for more and better parks for the public to enjoy, but Mr. White has not let his interest stop there. Emporia for many years had had two parks, each a block square, near the center of town. Each had a bandstand, benches, and shade trees and was fine for public meetings or band concerts in good weather, and each offered shady places where people could stop and rest, but they were not Mr. White's idea of a park. Soden's Grove, a large piece of private land more than a mile and a half from the center of town on the Cottonwood River, had a bandstand, a combination skating rink and dance pavilion for those who could afford to pay, and picnic tables among the big elm trees, but it was low ground which frequently flooded when the river came up, and this did not satisfy the Whites. Several miles northwest of town was Dryer

115

Park, named after a former city commissioner and built around the city reservoir. This was a fine picnic spot and adjoining it was a public golf course, a great attraction for those adults who did not belong to the Country Club. All these parks had a few swings, teeter-totters, and other simple playground pieces, but none was the recreational center of which the Whites dreamed.

For many years a high piece of ground between the southwest city limits and the Cottonwood River had appealed to the Whites as the site for a children's park, but never did they mention it in the paper. A few years after the death of their daughter, Mary, the Whites began quietly buying up bits of the ground, some of which had houses on them. Mr. White had to mortgage one of his downtown business properties to get all the land he wanted, but finally he acquired fifty acres and appeared before the city commissioners with a proposal which startled them as well as the whole population of Emporia.

The Whites offered to give this land to the city for a public park, but there were definite strings attached to the gift. It was these "ifs" which startled those who did not know the Whites so well, but to their intimate friends it was no surprise. While the park was to be a memorial to their daughter, Mary, it was not to be named for her. The conditions upon which the gift was to be made to the people of Emporia included:

That the name selected for the park have no connection with any member of the White family.

That the Whites be allowed to have landscape engineers plan the park, that it be laid out according to these plans, and that the Whites be permitted to improve the park as they saw fit, with all these expenses to be paid by the Whites.

That the park contain no roads or highways and that all vehicles be prohibited in the park.

That everything in the park be free and that at no time would anyone ever be able to sell anything within its boundaries.

The city might have been reluctant to accept such a large piece of land had all the improvements fallen on the city park fund, but under the conditions made by the Whites it was gladly accepted. The ground was set aside primarily as a children's playground and it was named Peter Pan Park, a name which I believe was suggested by Mrs. White, although no one ever found out definitely where it came from. Houses were cleared away and a Kansas City landscaping firm was employed. Two softball diamonds were laid out at one

117

end, while to the north among the trees were built six fine tennis courts and a playground, where the city since has installed much apparatus. A large lake was built by constructing a dam at the lower end of a natural draw and a drainage ditch, through which surface water from the south part of town poured, fed the lake, which filled quickly. Dutch ovens for cooking, stone tables, and benches were scattered through the park under the trees, and south of the tennis courts Mr. White's own idea was carried out. He had a large square of concrete poured and grapevines were planted to grow over trellises which covered the concrete. This, he planned, would be a fine place for dancing if the picnickers wanted to provide their own music, and in wet weather picnics could be held on the concrete. An ornamental gateway and a shelter house were built of native limestone in simple Grecian style and at intervals around the park were placed pillars of the same stone and structural lines.

Mr. and Mrs. Frank Reed, of Neosho, Mo., philanthropists who loved children and had built wading pools for them in towns near their home, heard of the park the Whites had built for Emporia's children and they built a $5,000 pool in Peter Pan Park, large enough to accommodate several hundred children at one time. The day of its dedication was a big one and it was estimated that between eight and ten thousand persons were at the park. The speeches were short, at the insistence of the Whites, but at the same time there were more dignitaries on the program than ever have appeared on the same bill in Emporia before or since. Among the honored guests were Vice-president Charles Curtis, United States Senator Arthur Capper, Congressman Homer Hoch, Governor Harry Woodring, and Federal Judge George McDermott.

The crowd gathered around the pool and Mr. White called for quiet by whistling a couple of times through his teeth, a trick he learned as a boy and now uses when he calls someone in the *Gazette* office and gets no response to his shouts. Then Vice-president Curtis lifted little Sallie Lindsay, a niece of Mr. and Mrs. White's, into the pool. Mr. White shouted "come and get it" and the children rushed for the pool. Trouble might have occurred, so many children were trying to use the pool at the same time, had not the word spread quickly that free ice cream was being served.

Another feature of the park, this one conceived and built by the Whites, is an amphitheater where every summer public shows are given by the Peter Pan Pageant Association, a volunteer organization to which

119

150 or 200 Emporians belong every year. Memberships range from one dollar upward and all the money is used for the shows, which are directed by F. L. Gilson, head of the dramatics department at Emporia State Teachers College, and in which actors and musicians from Teachers College, the College of Emporia, the city schools, and the town take part. Shakespearean plays, with musical introductions and interludes, were given the first few years, and last summer "In Our Town" was presented. Two performances are given each summer, one on Saturday night and the other on Sunday night, so that more persons from out of town can attend, and crowds have ranged from five to twelve thousand persons. The spectators sit on a natural grassy slope and watch the action on the stage, which is separated from the audience by a mirror pool and is eight stone steps higher than the pool. Simple stone columns are at each end of the stage and at intervals on the ends and back, while shrubs and huge elm trees form a natural background. While lights and sound systems are used, the productions are given entirely without scenery, depending on the narration, music, and costuming to put across the idea.

The idea of everything in the park being free still is carried out, although several refreshment stands operate just outside the park. Just east of the park is a public swimming pool, built and operated by J. H. Lawrence, who once was a country merchant in western Kansas. One of his children became afflicted with infantile paralysis and doctors told him exercise in water would help the child, so he built a small pool in his yard. Children of the neighbors liked to play in the pool, so he enlarged it and finally he gave up the mercantile business and moved to Ottawa, Kans., where, with a partner, he built a public pool. Then, hearing of Peter Pan Park and deciding it was an ideal place for a pool, he built the one in Emporia, later selling his Ottawa interest to his partner. The Emporia pool is the only one Lawrence owns today, but he operates under lease city-owned pools in half a dozen places in Kansas. Never forgetting how he got his start in the business and remembering what the water did for his daughter, Mr. Lawrence today urges infantile paralysis victims to use his pools free.

"A fine pool like that operated by a man like Mr. Lawrence is a great asset to a town and certainly it adds to Peter Pan Park," Mr. White told the city commissioners once when Lawrence was seeking a readjustment of water rates. "We should encourage many more businesses operated by men like him."

121

Every year the *Gazette* cooperates with the pool in a free learn-to-swim week. Mr. and Mrs. White drive around the park nearly every day in the summer, just to see that the children and adults are enjoying the facilities, but they never have stopped to watch a softball or tennis game. However, they have never missed one of the Peter Pan Pageants and they enjoy many picnics in the park, in certain times of the summer fighting chiggers along with other Emporians who have learned to enjoy outside recreation in spite of these little insects. Chiggers live on the grass and shrubs; they are almost too small to be seen but they leave red marks on the body which itch for several days. For days before the Peter Pan Pageant shows, Mr. White urges the people not only to attend but to take blankets or newspapers to sit on. Sulphur and various commercial chemicals, rubbed on the body, keep the bugs away and at times the pageant crowds have smelled like drug factories, but Kansans are accustomed to this and it does not bother them.

A nine-hole golf course, made on ground leased by the city and operated by the city on a fee and membership basis, adjoins Peter Pan Park on the west.

"This must be a fine thing," Mr. White once said, "because so many people use it. I'm glad it's there but

I couldn't tell a caddy from a putter and I'm glad I don't have to have anything to do with it."

Another park project in which Mr. White has taken the lead is a small tract of land at the extreme north end of Emporia, across the street from the Country Club. This park, originally sponsored and financed largely by the Rotary Club and Mr. White, is close to the better homes in Emporia, while Peter Pan Park, in the extreme south part of town, is in the district which some towns term "on the other side of the tracks." Peter Pan Park is south of the Santa Fe tracks which cross the town and is in that section populated by families in the lower income brackets, but Emporians never refer to this district as "across the tracks," and many of the leading citizens in civic and municipal affairs live in this section. The Reverend J. C. Brogan, pastor of the Grace Methodist Church, the membership of which is composed almost entirely of people from this district close to the railroad yards, was one of the most popular mayors Emporia ever had.

The Rotary Club and Mr. White bought most of the ground for the Rotary park, which has about ten acres and which officially is named Hammond Park, in honor of John Hammond, one of Emporia's first settlers. The Rotary Club has passed the hat fre-

123

quently among its membership in an effort to match money spent for the park by Mr. White, but he still is several jumps ahead of the club. The park, undeveloped for half a dozen years, now is being landscaped, and tennis courts, a softball diamond, bridges, and roads are being built by National Youth Administration labor with materials furnished by the city.

CHAPTER XII

THE "Y" IS SAVED

THE EMPORIA Y.M.C.A., A THREE-STORY brick building a block from the *Gazette* office and near the center of town, has been Mr. White's pride and joy but also a problem since its construction was started in 1915. The Y.M.C.A. had financial troubles from the start, and had it not been for Mr. White, who took the leadership in some vigorous financial campaigns, its doors would have closed long ago. And he has given money as well as leadership.

Many Emporians, especially those who have the money to contribute to various community enterprises, are not so keen about the "Y" as Mr. White is, and a good many men have told me they would not contribute to the organization if it were not for Mr. White.

"It does some good, but not nearly so much as the same money would do if used in some other ways and I wouldn't give a dime if it weren't for your boss," said one businessman, who is a close friend of Mr. White. "Frankly, I wish it would close."

"Why don't you tell Mr. White that, instead of me?" I suggested. "He's the one who is keeping it open."

"I wouldn't tell him for anything," the merchant replied. "His heart and soul are wrapped up in it and if he wants it, I guess we'll just have to support it. Lord knows he's done enough for the town that if he wants us to kick in a little on one of his hobbies, he has it coming to him."

A few others did not take such a friendly attitude. They admitted to everyone except Mr. White that they were not friendly to the project and that they wished the "Y" would close, but they did not feel like publicly opposing anything Mr. White wanted.

Mr. White called a meeting in 1914 and explained to the men who attended that he believed Emporia should have a Y.M.C.A. with a modern building for the youths of the town. Those at the meeting were agreeable and Mr. White made the motion that an organization be formed. But the World War was developing across the ocean, people in this country felt things were uncertain, and Emporians decided to wait until after the war for their Y.M.C.A., most of them believing the war would end in a few months. But in 1915 the war was still progressing and Emporians, deciding to go ahead, adopted plans, let a contract for the "Y" building, and staged a big financial drive, of which Mr. White was the head. The cornerstone was laid in April, 1916, the building was finished in February of 1917, and a gala celebration was held for the opening of the Y.M.C.A., complete in every detail, even to a $40,000 mortgage. That would be easy to pay since much of the money was pledged, thought the Emporians, but they soon found themselves buying Liberty bonds, and the urgency of the "Y" debt was slighted in the excitement of war.

The end of the war found the Y.M.C.A. a busy place, but still with a $40,000 mortgage hanging over it. Some Emporians who had pledged large amounts had moved away and others had died. For years the organization had a struggle, annual campaigns netting only enough to meet current expenses, pay the interest on the mortgage, and possibly a little of the principal. During all these years Mr. White was on the board of the "Y" and Mrs. White worked on the women's division teams during the financial drives.

At the luncheon meeting of the "Y" directors in the building, the board was discussing the financial prob-

127

lems while a women's society of a church was preparing luncheon. Long past the luncheon time, the problems had not been solved and the men were getting hungry, when one of the women tiptoed in and whispered to the "Y" secretary. He slipped out of the room and in a few minutes returned to announce that the city had shut off the organization's water supply because the bill had not been paid and that the women could not finish the meal without water. Several members of the board went to a private home in the neighborhood and got buckets of water while the other directors, including Mr. White, passed the hat and raised enough money to pay the water bill.

By 1938 only half of the mortgage had been paid. The mortgage holders wanted money and agreed to settle for half of the $20,000 owed them, but the building was run down and the organization had no money for repairs, to say nothing of the mortgage. It was now or never, the directors agreed, so a campaign with a definite time limit was launched to raise $15,000, which would pay the mortgage holders fifty cents on the dollar and provide $5,000 for building repairs. "Y" workers worked as they never had worked before and the goal was in sight, but the day set for the end of the campaign found the goal $4,000 short. Deter-

At His Birthday Party in 1938, Mr. White Tells His Old
Friend Henry Allen, Former Kansas Governor and U. S. Senator,
How It Feels to Be Seventy.

mined not to close the "Y," Mr. White volunteered to raise the money himself. He pleaded with his friends, he called on everyone he thought could give, and he wrote letters to heads of large business organizations which had branches in Emporia. For years he had been a member of the "special gifts" committee in the annual drives, soliciting those most able to give large amounts, and he had long been writing letters to the home offices of chain stores, asking help in the Emporia campaigns. His pleas, however, brought only $1,500, and the doors of the Y.M.C.A. were locked.

"It was the best I could do," he said in an editorial in the *Gazette,* in which he recalled his boyhood days when the river was his swimming pool and the barn loft his gymnasium and when a boy had so many chores to do that he needed no "Y" or public playground. "I felt it was my duty. I had started the thing. I had worked for it all these years. I believed in it. I still think it has a real function. I appealed to my friends for help. Because they differed with me honestly, they turned me down. I failed. It's all right. I'm not unhappy about it. At least I was not a quitter. I made the first motion to open the Y.M.C.A. and I made the last motion—to close it—and that episode is closed. On the whole I am sure the town has been

129

better and I am sure I have been better for the twenty-five years I spent with the 'Y.' And what ghosts flit about its walls for me. While young men see visions, may we not dream dreams?"

It was an editorial of complete humiliation, and, while I am certain the words came straight from the editor's heart, I also believe that he felt such a piece might be the spark that would set off some kind of a miracle. And it did.

Weeks before, a large chain business organization had been solicited for help through its officials. No reply had been received to Mr. White's plea for funds. But finally the letter found its way to an officer who had spent his boyhood doing chores in a small town, swimming in the river, and performing on a home-made trapeze as Mr. White had done. About the time the letter reached his desk, he also read in the *Gazette*, to which the company subscribed for advertising checking purposes, Mr. White's editorial on the closing of the Y.M.C.A.

There was the spark that kindled a new fire. The business official mailed Mr. White a good-sized check for the "Y" and wrote: "Thanks for the editorial and the memories it revived. And thanks for your fight to save the 'Y.'"

130

That letter and gift were all Emporia Y.M.C.A. workers needed for another inspiration, and they started out again. No gift was too small to be considered and within a few weeks the last of the money was raised. The "Y" was repaired and reopened and a public dinner was held in the Y.M.C.A. gymnasium, at which Mr. White scratched a match on the seat of his pants and burned the mortgage while several hundred men and women stood and sang the Doxology.

"I was afraid for a minute when I looked at the mortgage I was holding before the crowd," Mr. White told me afterward. "Not afraid for the 'Y' but for myself. I hadn't scratched a match on the seat of my pants for years and I didn't want to fail this time. That mortgage was made back in the days when he-men always scratched their matches on their hindquarters. Only sissies used the soles of their shoes."

The College of Emporia has been another of the things for which Mr. White has worked continually. Although he belongs to the Congregational church, he has given thousands of dollars to the Presbyterian college and has worked hard as a member of its board and on its various financial campaigns. This winter, even while he was literally swamped with work as chairman of the Committee to Defend America by

131

Aiding the Allies, he has been helping the College of Emporia in a desperate fight to raise enough money to pay its debts and keep its doors open.

Although Mr. White has been a member of the Chamber of Commerce since its organization more than twenty-five years ago, he never has held office in it, not even as a board member. He frequently attends meetings of both the board and the membership when something of civic importance is coming up and often he is a speaker at public meetings arranged by the chamber. He usually is asked to introduce distinguished speakers and other guests at Chamber of Commerce and other civic affairs and he never refuses if he can fill the date. While the *Gazette* holds six memberships in the Chamber of Commerce and is one of its largest financial supporters, employees of the *Gazette* do not hold offices in the organization, other than a directorship. One member of the *Gazette* force usually is on the Chamber of Commerce board and several times a *Gazette* man has been suggested as vice-president or president, but he has always nipped the suggestion in the bud. There is no rule laid down by Mr. White that a *Gazette* man cannot take such an office, but Mr. White has refused

132

through the years and his men have followed his example.

"We can do just as much working as individuals," he says, "and if one of us had an office people would get the idea we were trying to run the organization. Good workers are more scarce than men who want office."

CHAPTER XIII

AN EYE FOR BUSINESS

I HAVE OFTEN HEARD IT SAID THAT MR. White is an editor and not a businessman and that he does not know anything about the business end of his newspaper. The men and women in the *Gazette* office know better and more Emporians are learning it all the time. In the first place, the editor has not forgotten his youthful days as printer and he knows good printing. As he scans *Gazette* editions as they roll off the press, he looks at the printing as well as the text of the news stories, features, and advertising, and if a page has been printed poorly, a picture does not show up well, or something else has gone wrong, he immediately goes through the office with his paper until he finds out if the thing has been corrected. He likes a clear print with plenty of impression put on the type and enough ink used to make the text and art work black. Many times I have seen him grab a paper out of a bundle of the first copies brought from the pressroom, glance at the paper, and then march—not walk, but march—right down to the pressroom to talk to the pressman personally. And he always stays until the papers rolling off the press are black enough to please him.

Mr. White reads the advertising in his paper, and, to let the merchants know that he does, he frequently goes out on the street on shopping expeditions, stopping at one store after another, buying groceries, meat, household articles, clothing, and hardware. Naturally the White household cannot use all the things he buys, and many times the deliverymen have left packages at homes of *Gazette* employees which were mysteries until it developed that the boss had had them sent out.

Groceries and meats are his specialties. He is likely to drop into any foodstore which advertises, pick out a few articles, and have them sent home, after giving the whole store a quick "once-over." Much food is consumed at the White home, for there are many guests, but even then there is sometimes a problem as a result of the editor's shopping sprees.

"Don't these things he has sent out upset your menu schedule?" I asked Miss Bertha Colglazier, the Whites' housekeeper, in the kitchen one evening after several

Gazette men and their wives had been guests to help eat a big beef roast Mr. White had bought.

"It used to worry me," she replied, "but I got used to it. Look here and I'll show you something."

She led the way into the pantry and opened the refrigerator and there was a beef roast about the same size as the one we had had for dinner.

"I ordered that one yesterday for dinner tonight. Then Mr. White stopped in a store on the way home and ordered another and that's what you got, but we'll eat the other eventually," grinned the housekeeper, drying her hands and hanging up the dish towel less than five minutes after the dinner was over. Menus, even with Mr. White's extra purchases, are no problem for this kitchen manager, who can cook a meal, serve it to from eight to a dozen persons, and get all the china and silver washed and dried before the people in the dining room have finished with the next course.

Leaders—merchandise which the storekeepers advertise and sell at cost or below cost to get people into their stores—are constant worries of the Emporia editor, who believes that every businessman is entitled to a fair profit on what he sells.

"But we must have leaders," a grocer told him. "People insist on bargains."

"All right, if you must, you must," replied Mr. White, picking out half a dozen cantaloupes to be sent out to his home. "But why in the name of good business do you make leaders out of staple goods—sugar, flour, shortening, potatoes—the things people have to eat? You grocers should get together and confine your leaders to the fancy things—jars of pickles, jellies and jams, prepared noodles, or prepared desserts—those things which might be classed as luxuries."

A few weeks later all the grocery and meat dealers were invited to a luncheon at the Broadview Hotel. Mr. White wanted to tell all of them at the same time what he had told the one dealer when I heard him and what he probably had told most of them individually. At the luncheon most of the food dealers agreed that Mr. White was right, but no one offered any kind of agreement for adoption. Some of the worst offenders at cutting prices of staple merchandise had not attended the luncheon and those present did not believe such an agreement could be unanimous.

"Well, it's your show," the editor told them before he dismissed the meeting. "I can tell you how I think you should run your business, but I can't run it for you. But I do know this—you have to make money to stay in business and if you don't stay in business, I

137

don't get your advertising business. But you know better than I do what you can and can't do."

Another time Emporia had a bread war and none of the bakeries was making any money. Mr. White, through C. C. Alexander of the advertising office, arranged a meeting of the bakery managers, and before the thing ended several meetings were held. The result was a uniform loaf of bread at the same price. The bakers ignored the fact that a cut-rate chain store was shipping in bread and selling it much cheaper.

The Emporia editor's theory on bargains was summed up in one editorial which was printed on Apr. 14, 1932, and was reprinted in newspapers and trade journals all over the country.

"Last week we had a Dollar Day in Emporia, and thousands of dollars were spent on Commercial Street by buyers who found genuine bargains," he wrote. "These bargain days and dollar days furnish occasions when merchants can clean up their stocks, thin overcrowded lines, get rid of odds and ends that have not been selling well but which are good material sold at a narrow margin, and on the whole, everything considered, are sold upon a commercially wise policy, even if at a low profit. The bargain days and the special days are legitimate commercial vehicles for disposing of honest goods in a wise transaction profitable to the buyer and the seller.

"Having said which the *Gazette* now desires to talk to the buyers and the merchants of this town about another entirely different tendency, the tendency to go 'cheap,' to sell, not seasonally once or twice a year but day in and day out, cheap stuff at cheap prices, promoting transactions which do neither side of the bargain any great good.

"The *Gazette* has a larger interest in this community than that which goes with the immediate dollar. It is easy to grab off the immediate dollar, the quick, more or less dirty dollar in advertising, but the *Gazette* expects to be running here on something like the same management for the next quarter of a century. Hence we feel licensed to talk to advertisers and buyers alike and advise them to begin considering quality.

"In the subsidence of wealth all over this world in the past four years, buyers have been looking for things that would merely piece out—which means cheap things at cheap prices. All the world is going cheap. Incidentally it is going busted while going cheap. Forty years ago Benjamin Harrison lost the presidency by saying that 'a cheap coat makes a cheap man.' But it is true just the same. Cheap mer-

139

chandising makes cheap people. By cheap, we mean shoddy, makeshift, pretend-to-be, just-as-good substitutes, second- and third-grade stuff. Quality costs but it lasts, and in the end quality is cheaper than shoddy.

"Now a word to the advertisers. You can't make any money selling goods at a loss. 'Leaders' do not get you anywhere. In the first place, shoppers come and buy your leaders priced at a loss and leave your store and go after the other things where they know they can get values. And the more money you sacrifice drawing crowds to your store by leaders priced below cost, the sooner there is going to be a cloth sign tacked over your front door which reads: 'Selling out at cost' or 'Bankrupt Sale' or 'Removal Sale.' In the second place, cheap merchandise threatens your good will. When your customer realizes you sold him something cheap, which proved unsatisfactory, that customer will resent it and trade elsewhere in the future. Carry quality goods, advertise quality goods—goods that you can stand back of as represented—make a low profit above overhead expense, but make a profit. That does not mean we cannot hold bargain sales now and then to reduce stocks and clean out odds and ends. Dollar days and special sales based on store needs for new goods are wholesome.

140

"And now for the community. Remember this: Cheap merchandising makes a cheap community. In Atchison in the last year ten stores have closed, some in failure. Why? Because merchants thought they could make money on leaders priced below cost and they got something started they could not stop. When everybody prices a different leader, the whole merchandising structure of a town is on a minus cost basis and sooner or later the bats fly in at the windows of that town, the coyotes run in the streets, and the sheriff's auctioneer is the town's merchant.

"Emporia cannot afford to go cheap. Somewhat it is the business of the merchants to see that it doesn't: but largely this is the business of the buyer. For every penny you save on cheap stuff your town sinks that much lower and your property is cut down that much. Cheap merchandising soon is reflected in vacant buildings. Vacant buildings bring lower rent. Lower rent brings lower real estate values. Up come the cloth signs and down goes the town.

"We have thought a long time before writing this editorial. We of the *Gazette* are in the same boat with the merchants. We could jam the paper full of advertising of cheap merchandise sold at a loss. And the merchants would make a minute daily balance—not

141

'profit on sales of cheap leaders.' But ten years from now with 5,000 off the population where would the *Gazette* be? Where would we all be? This is a serious matter for Emporians who are here to stay.

"A cheap town makes a cheap, quick funeral."

CHAPTER XIV

POLITICALLY MINDED

M R. WHITE HAS BEEN INTERESTED IN politics ever since he can remember. As a child he heard politics discussed at home by his father, the loyal Democrat, and his mother, a staunch Republican. The political rallies and the torchlight parades were the shows he enjoyed in his youth, long before he began his newspaper career, in which most men become politically minded to some extent. As a reporter and editorial writer for other newspapers, he wrote political news and opinion, so it was only natural that, when he purchased the *Gazette* in 1895, as an editor he should make politics one of his chief editorial topics. But there his interest in his community and his state—all the people around him—predominated and his interest in politics was not for the party, but for the benefits the people could derive from the party.

Luck threw the Emporian into national politics and

143

national fame just as it got him into the newspaper business. In the summer of 1896, Mr. and Mrs. White were getting ready for a vacation in Estes Park, Colo., and the editor was trying to write enough editorials to fill the column while he was away, with the few he planned to write during his vacation and mail home. Returning to his office from the post office the afternoon he and Mrs. White were to leave on a train, he was stopped by a local Populist, whose identity Mr. White does not even remember today, and a political discussion followed, with the editor taking the side of the Republican party in the heated McKinley-Bryan campaign. A small crowd gathered around the two men on the sidewalk near the *Gazette* office and the discussion grew more heated, with the majority arguing on the side of the Populist, who favored Bryan's campaign of cheap money. Remembering he had work to do and had to catch a train that afternoon, Mr. White broke away from the argument while it was at its peak and he was still "boiling" when he sat down to write another editorial. The result was "What's the Matter with Kansas?", a scathing piece pointing out how Kansas had in the past few years lost in population, capital, and general prestige over the country. He flayed the Democratic followers and attributed to them the general run-down condition of Kansas, although fifteen years later, in an introduction to a reprint in booklet form of his editorial, Mr. White admitted that Kansas had had a series of droughts and bad crop years before 1896 and that the Populists were not entirely to blame for things.

However, while he still was excited over the street argument, he wrote "What's the Matter with Kansas?", which in his own mind did not have any special significance and was merely a repetition of the things he had said during his argument. With other editorials he had written before starting the vacation, "What's the Matter with Kansas?" appeared in the *Gazette* and in some way got to Chicago, where it was reprinted by a Republican paper. New York papers picked it up; Mark Hanna, chairman of the Republican National Committee, read it and had it reprinted by the thousands for distribution over the country. Mr. White returned from his vacation several weeks later and discovered he was politically famous. Following the McKinley victory, the Emporian was asked what he wanted out of the political pie and he astonished party leaders by declaring firmly that he wanted nothing, that he had no desire for any office. Shortly afterward Mr. White went East and with him went a

145

letter of introduction to President-elect McKinley, signed by Hanna. The letter, which now hangs in a frame over his desk in Mr. White's *Gazette* office, follows:

Feb. 12-97.

Hon. Wm. McKinley:
My dear Sir:

This will introduce Mr. W. A. White who wrote What's the Matter with Kansas. I have a great admiration for this young man and bespeak for him your kind consideration. He wants no office.

Sincerely yours

M. A. Hanna.

Thousands of times since then, Mr. White has looked at the letter as he has sat at his desk, dictating editorials which shaped his political policies, as he has advised young men with promising ability in the business world not to follow politics as a career, and as he has consoled one-time political war horses who have fallen by the roadside in the political race.

Since that time Mr. White has been a prominent figure in national affairs, not only in party politics but in governmental, educational, humane, philanthropic, and many other organizations. He always has

146

been partisan, supporting the Republican party except in 1912, when he was a prominent factor in the presidential campaign of his good friend Theodore Roosevelt on the Progressive ticket. But the Emporia editor has not been so party-minded that he could see no fault in his own party and no good in the others. At times his support of his own party has seemed halfhearted, so much credit has he given candidates on other tickets. But it never has worried him. The campaign of 1940 was one of those times when Republicans were not sure Mr. White was really for Wendell Willkie, so often did he commend Roosevelt, especially on his attitude toward foreign affairs in relation to the countries at war. But the Republican ticket was carried under the masthead of the *Gazette* and I know he and Mrs. White voted a straight ticket, from president on down to the local constable, except for district judge. In that case young Joe Rolston, Democrat, was the only candidate. Even the Republicans in the three counties in the district thought Rolston was the best man for the job and no one ran against him.

While he has helped write national Republican party platforms, has made many speeches for national committees, has been delegate to national political conventions, and has been an intimate friend of presi-

147

dents, Mr. White has sought only one political office because he wanted the office. That job is Republican committeeman in his local precinct, a district of about thirty square blocks with a few hundred voters, most of whom generally vote Republican. That is a job he likes, and he attends county Republican meetings and takes part in their affairs with great interest. He has held the office several years. In 1912 he ran and was elected Republican national committeeman for Kansas, more because he wanted to defeat David W. Mulvane than because he wanted the office. Soon after he was elected, he resigned to become national committeeman of the Progressive party. He became a member of the Progressive party's executive committee under Theodore Roosevelt and he stayed with the party until its convention dissolved it in 1916.

Only once in all his political career has Mr. White been a candidate for any office other than that of committeeman in his own party, and that time, when he ran for governor of Kansas on the independent anti-Ku Klux Klan ticket in 1924, he worked for votes sixteen hours every day and worried in his sleep the other eight hours in fear of what he would have to do if he were elected. Although he was not elected, he polled one vote of every four cast, and he got more votes in

Kansas than John W. Davis, Democratic candidate for president, got with all his organization and party prestige.

Always against religious and racial prejudices, Mr. White lost no time in "jumping on" the Klan when it was revived in Kansas early in 1921. When the first organizer came to town in July of 1921, the *Gazette's* editor began writing editorials against the Klan and its program, and *Gazette* reporters were prying into the Klan's secret meetings and printing stories about who attended. In the next three years several *Gazette* reporters were threatened by delegations from the Klan. Having been rather roughly ejected from several Klan meetings which I had managed to attend somehow or other, I know full well the hatred the organization held for Mr. White and his paper.

"To make a case against a birthplace, a religion, or a race is wicked, un-American, and cowardly," was one of the nicer things Mr. White wrote about the Klan in his editorial campaign against it. Among other things he called it was "a self-constituted body of moral idiots who would substitute the findings of the Ku Klux Klan for the processes of law." Another time he wrote: "It is an organization of traitors to American institutions," a few sentences later adding: "The Ku

Klux Klan in this community is a menace to peace
and decent neighborly living, and if we find out who
is the Imperial Wizard in Emporia we shall guy the
life out of him. He is a joke, you may be sure. But
a poor joke at that."

We never did find out for sure who the Imperial
Wizard was—if that was the title of the head man—but
we did know many of the Klan leaders and members,
and the *Gazette* printed their names in connection
with the campaign against the "kluxers," as the *Gazette* called them, using a little *k*. When the Klan was
going its best, Emporia elected a mayor who admitted
he was a member, and a half a dozen others went into
city and courthouse offices with the support of the
Klan and did not denounce it. A few boldly admitted
they were members and these few received better
treatment at the hands of the *Gazette* than those who
would neither admit nor deny membership. For more
than three months not one *Gazette* reporter could get
a news item out of the police office. No one in au-
thority would even talk to the reporters. Police Judge
J. H. J. Rice, who was pastor of the First Congregational Church, of which Mr. White was a member,
kept the paper informed of what was going on after
events reached his court. When I came back to the

Gazette after spending a year as a reporter for the *Kansas City Star*, I was put on the police run and was admitted to the building and given the news. For some reason I never knew, the Klansmen would rather fight with me than ignore me and from then on as long as the Klan held the reins of the city, the *Gazette* got the news, but I was in and out of hot water all day long.

Only once did I have any serious trouble with the Klan. One of the first days Emporia's new seven-story Broadview Hotel was open, two groups took up about all the rooms. One group was composed of about fifty or sixty members of a foreign musical organization which was giving a concert in town that night. All the men had high-heeled shoes, long hair, and foreign names. The other group was composed of delegates to a state convention of the Klan. Realizing the readers could tell which belonged to each group, Mr. White sent me to the hotel to copy the names of all guests from the hotel register. While I was doing it, one of the Klansmen tried to take the list away from me. We were wrestling around the lobby and a few fists had just begun to fly when the hotel manager came in and demanded to know what was going on. At his request, I gave him the list I had copied, although I argued

151

that hotel registry lists were public property. I returned to the office and told the story to Mr. White, who immediately wrote a short note for me to deliver to one of the directors of the hotel corporation. "Read it on the way over," he told me. The note, which was so short that it made no sense to the hotel director until I told him what had gone on before, read:

"If a copy of the Broadview Hotel register for today is not in our office by seven o'clock this evening, the name of the Broadview never again will be printed in the *Gazette* except in case of police raids and similar events.—W. A. WHITE."

The next day was a holiday, when the *Gazette* always puts out a morning rather than an evening paper. About six o'clock that evening, while we were working on the morning edition, in walked the manager of the hotel. Wrapped in a newspaper he carried, not a list of the names on the register, but the hotel register itself. We copied the names and in the paper we printed them under a paragraph stating that the hotel had been filled for the first time, with two groups, the foreign musicians and the kluxer delegates, taking most of the rooms. In the same paper we carried an editorial written by Mr. White, stating what a fine hotel the Broadview was and how much it meant to the town. As he dropped the copy into the basket on the city editor's desk, he said: "Always remember after you spank a child, you should give it a piece of candy. It makes everyone feel better." The *Gazette* and the hotel have been good friends ever since.

In September, 1924, after Jonathan M. Davis, the Democratic incumbent, and Ben S. Paulen, the Republican candidate, had been nominated for governor, Mr. White decided that since both of them had been endorsed by the Klan and had not disclaimed it, he would run for governor as an independent. The Republican party council before the primary that year was divided on the Klan issue. Paulen, on the resolutions committee, defeated an anti-Klan resolution and went before the party's state council and prevented even a debate on the Klan on the floor of the convention. Republican newspapers, which predominate in Kansas, urged Paulen to denounce the Klan, but he refused. When he was accused of being a Klansman, he denied it, but he always used the phrase "at this time."

Most leaders in the Democratic party also were against the Klan, but Jonathan Davis refused to denounce it and he was running with the hearty endorsement of Democratic Klansmen.

153

"I have filed my petition for governor and am in this race to win," Mr. White wrote in his announcement. "It is the largest independent petition ever filed for an office in Kansas. Over three times more names were signed to these petitions for Carl Taylor and myself for lieutenant governor and governor than were needed. None of these petitions came from my home town or county. I wished honestly to test sentiment. There can be no doubt about this sentiment. The issue in Kansas this year is the Ku Klux Klan above everything. The Ku Klux Klan is found in nearly every county. It represents a small minority of the citizenship and it is organized for purposes of terror. Its terror is directed at law-abiding citizens, Negroes, Jews, and Catholics. These groups in Kansas comprise more than a fourth of our population. They are entitled to their full constitutional rights; their rights to life, liberty, and the pursuit of happiness. They menace no one. They are good citizens—law-abiding, God-fearing, prosperous, patriotic. Yet because of their skin, their race, or their creed, the Ku Klux Klan in Kansas is subjecting them to economic boycott, to social ostracism, to every form of harassment, annoyance, and every terror that a bigoted minority can use. And the leaders of the two major parties in this

154

state lift no hand to help them. . . . I want to be
governor to free Kansas from the disgrace of the Ku
Klux Klan. And I want to offer Kansans afraid of the
Klan and ashamed of that disgrace, a candidate who
shares their fear and shame. So I am in the race to
stay and to win. . . . The thought that Kansas should
have a government beholden to this hooded gang of
masked fanatics, ignorant and tyrannical in their ruth-
less oppression, is what calls me out of the pleasant
ways of my life into this distasteful but necessary task.
I cannot sit idly by and see Kansas become a byword
among the states.

"I call to my support least of all those who are op-
pressed by the Ku Klux Klan. We must have no class
issue here. I call to my support rather all fair-minded
citizens of every party, of every creed, to stop the oppression of this minority of our people. It is a nation-
wide menace, this Klan. It knows no party. It knows
no country. It knows only bigotry, malice, and terror.
Our national government is founded on reason and
the Golden Rule. This Klan is preaching and practic-
ing terror and force. Its only prototype is the Soviet
of Russia. So I feel that I am walking the path of duty
in going into this race. I ask my fellow Kansans to
come with me and to stand with me for free govern-

155

ments and the righteous guarantees of our constitution to all its citizens."

Mr. White had no state or county committees and he made his own speaking engagements in his six weeks' campaign in which he traveled 2,700 miles in his car, with Mrs. White or their son, Bill, always with him. He spent $75 for postage, most of it for sending out his petitions and getting them returned, and his only other expenses were for gasoline, oil, tires, meals, hotel bills, and repair bills for his old Dodge touring car.

Election day he worked at the *Gazette* as usual, but when evening came, the polls closed, and the vote counting began, he did not stay at the office with the force to watch the returns as usual. He went home for dinner, retired at eight o'clock, and did not know that Paulen was first, Davis second, and he third until he got the morning paper off his front porch at breakfast time.

"You can't watch me, because I'm going to bed," Mr. White said early election night to a reporter from the *Kansas City Star,* who had been sent here to write about Mr. White's activities on election night. "I have made my fight for what I believe and I'm tired and going to sleep in my own bed for the first night in weeks. Don't you dare call me to tell me anything or ask me anything."

Within a year the Klan had practically died out in Kansas. Dr. Hiram Evans, the Imperial Wizard of the organization, announced a series of addresses in the state, and Mr. White welcomed him with the following editorial:

"Dr. Hiram Evans, the Imperial Wizard of the kluxers, is bringing his consecrated shirttail to Kansas this spring, and from five gloomy klaverns will make five Kansas speeches. We welcome him. Enter the wizard; sound the bull roarers and hewgags. Beat the tom-toms. He will see what was once a thriving and profitable hate factory and bigotorium now laughed into a busted community; where the cockeyed he-dragon wails for its first-born and the nightshirts of a once salubrious pageantry sag in the spring breezes and bag at the wabbly knees. The kluxers in Kansas are as dejected and sad as a last year's bird-nest, afflicted with general debility, dizziness on going upstairs, and general aversion to female society!"

That ended the Klan in Kansas.

CHAPTER XV

EMPORIA COMES FIRST

WHILE MR. WHITE APPEARS FRE-
quently in the national political picture, taking part in conferences, caucuses, and committee meetings, as well as writing political stories, he is as much
if not more interested in local politics. The courthouse, he believes, is the foundation of government
and when the people cease to use good judgment in
the election of county officers, they are likely to grow
careless in the selection of higher officers.

He likes to see good men in office, but on the other
hand he hates for the individual's sake to see men who
could do well in private life run for office. I have heard
him tell prospective candidates that too often a man
thinks he will hold office only a short time to get a
start or until he can get something else, but, once in
office, he gets the political bug in his system and cannot keep from seeking political jobs.

When his son, W. L. White, then associate editor

of the *Gazette,* ran for the state legislature in 1930, I know Mr. White did not exactly approve of it, but I never heard him tell Bill not to run. I think the father thought that one term would get the urge to hold office out of Bill's system, and apparently it did, for he did not seek reelection and has not been a candidate for anything since then. On the other hand, Mr. White did believe that a term in the legislature, which meant living with the politicians in Topeka for several months, would give Bill a view of political life that would help him later to understand better both how to do and how not to do things. I drove with Mr. and Mrs. White to Topeka to see Bill take the oath as a legislator, and immediately after the oath was given we all had luncheon, left Bill, and returned to Emporia. I believe that is the only time Mr. White has been in the legislative halls in the twenty years I have known him.

In the Kansas primary, in which both major parties nominate their county, district, state, and national candidates for the general election, Mr. White rarely does much for any individual candidate for county office. The exception is when one candidate is head and shoulders above the others for the job, and then it is only for Republican candidates that he works. He lets the Democrats run their primary without any praise or criticism from him. But after the primary, the picture changes suddenly. As soon as the primary votes are counted and the winners are determined, the list of Republican candidates from one end of the ticket to the other goes under the *Gazette's* masthead. During the campaign, each candidate gets one or more editorials, depending upon the qualifications of the candidate, the opposition he has, and how vital Mr. White thinks the race is.

Far too often the Republicans nominate poor candidates, and Mr. White recognizes them as quickly as anyone else does. But even these men and women get a spot in the editorial column at least once during the campaign and on these occasions Mr. White literally damns them with faint praise. He can, when he tries, write a two or three hundred word editorial about a candidate that pleases the candidate and his friends and at the same time makes the opponent and his friends feel good. Analyzed closely, these editorials say practically nothing.

When any candidate announces for office—no matter what his politics—Mr. White has a rule that the paper give the candidate a free story. His picture is printed if the candidate pays all the costs of the photography and engraving. Anything else the candidates want said about them—except for the Republican editorials—comes under political advertising, of which the *Gazette* gets a liberal amount from both parties. Emporia's only Democratic paper—and the *Gazette's* only newspaper competition—is a weekly with limited circulation, and often the Democrats advertise in the *Gazette* more than do the Republicans.

While Mr. White is writing editorials about the Republican candidates during campaigns, the Democrats are not neglected. Each campaign the *Gazette* gives the Democrats a column of space two or three times a week to extol the virtues of the Democrats and run down the Republicans. Sometimes a lot of this space is spent criticizing Mr. White as well as the Republican ticket, but the editor reads it and prints it. At the top of each Democratic column is a statement that the views and opinions which follow are those of the editor of the column, who is chosen by the Democratic county chairman with the approval of the *Gazette,* and are not the views and opinions of the *Gazette* or its editor. The *Gazette* has never said "No" to any Democratic column editor the party chairman has suggested, but usually the *Gazette* suggests names of Democrats

161

who the *Gazette* believes will conduct a decent campaign.

This Democratic column, Mr. White believes, does the Republicans as much good as it does the Democrats, for it brings the issues before the public and helps to kill whispering campaigns and the fact that the column is free to the Democrats lets the readers know that while the *Gazette* is partisan, it is not unfair.

"The Wailing Place," the *Gazette's* public forum column, which is printed every day there are any letters for it, is wide open during political campaigns, except that contributors must sign their names, which are printed with the letters, and they must abide by the rules of libel and decency. When severe charges are made against any person, the charges are shown to him before they are printed and he has an opportunity to have his answer in the same issue with the charges. "The Wailing Place" runs throughout the year in the *Gazette* and, except on special occasions, contributors are confined to five "wails" of 350 words each in a year. This rule was made to discourage a few individuals who contributed too much too often. They wrote more, Mr. White thought, to see their stuff printed than to better any cause.

The name, "The Wailing Place," was selected by Mr. White and despite much argument by contributors and readers, he refuses to change it. Some persons contend that "wailing" implies complaining and they do not like to be put in that light. But Mr. White believes it is a name which attracts attention and thus is a good one, and most of the letters which are submitted for the column are of a complaining nature.

Mr. White is a prohibitionist in practice as well as in theory. I have never seen him take a drink, although I have been with him at conventions and other meetings many times when liquor was served. I have even had drinks in his presence, in places where they were legal and when I was not going to drive a car soon afterward, and he never has said a word to me about it. He has no idea that a man who takes a drink is committing a moral sin and will go to hell, but he does think that liquor is a waste of money and that a person who takes many drinks lays himself open to forming a habit which can become an economic sin as well as tear down the drinker's moral, mental, and physical condition, thus often making drinking immoral. Mr. White cannot understand how a man can spend money on liquor when he might use the money for his family, which often is neglected because of the liquor.

163

Mr. White has been a prohibitionist all his life, and so sincere is he in his belief that he sticks to it even if it costs him money. Late in 1921 Mr. White was given a contract to write the editorials for *Judge,* the old weekly comic magazine. He was to receive, I was told at the time, $500 a week for two small magazine pages of editorials, and I know he was happy at the time, which was soon after the First World War, when money was scarce. The *Gazette* needed some new equipment and the money from *Judge* would help, it was explained. But after a few weeks, the agreement was broken. The editors of *Judge* favored the repeal of enough of the prohibition law to permit beer and light wines. Mr. White could not agree and he quit work for the magazine. He refused to sanction any form of repeal and gave up his work rather than write for something in which he did not believe.

While he did not change his opinion on the liquor question when states were ratifying or turning down the Twenty-first Amendment to the United States Constitution, which repealed the Eighteenth or Prohibition Amendment, Mr. White did favor a vote on the question in Kansas. And while he supported a vote on the question, he wrote editorials advocating prohibition of hard liquors. At the same time, he reversed the opinion which made him quit the job with *Judge* and he favored legalizing 3.2 per cent beer in Kansas. He explained his change in attitude by saying he still believed all alcoholic drinks were harmful, but that 3.2 beer was the least harmful of all and that, if Kansas permitted the low-voltage beer, it might prevent the repeal of the entire prohibition law in Kansas. At the time he predicted that if 3.2 per cent beer were permitted, much would be drunk at first and then the volume consumed would fall off. He was right. The sale of beer in Kansas in 1940 took a big drop over the preceding year, as the state records show.

Many persons who had been drinking hard liquor, much of which was made in abandoned coal mines in Southeast Kansas and bootlegged all over the state, would be satisfied with 3.2 per cent beer, Mr. White believed. For a time that was correct and beer sales were high, but as beer sales have decreased the sale of bootleg hard liquor has increased. Today bootleggers are thriving all over Kansas, even in Emporia, which is known as one of Kansas's driest towns. Many persons who do not buy from bootleggers bring their own liquor into the state from wet Missouri, Nebraska, and Colorado, most of that being consumed in Emporia com-

165

ing from Kansas City, Mo., only a little over a hundred miles away.

This year the Kansas legislature considered legislation to let the people vote again on the repeal of the state's prohibition law and the authorizing of state liquor stores. Mr. White was vacationing in Arizona with Mrs. White and made no comment on the proposal. While he may be for letting the people vote again, there is no doubt that he will again work to keep the prohibition law if it ever comes to a vote.

While much hard liquor is consumed in Kansas, its laws are drastic, and possession of any amount of liquor containing more than 3.2 per cent alcohol by volume is prohibited. The penalty is a minimum fine of $100 or a thirty-day jail sentence or both. A drunk with a stomach full of liquor, but none in a bottle or on his premises or in his car, is subject to a fine of a few dollars or a light jail sentence, and this fact leads the average Kansan, when he gets any liquor, to drink it all as quickly as possible. For this reason, Kansas has many drunks and drunken drivers. A drunken driver is subject only to the penalty for that offense, but if a man, either drunk or sober, has a bottle of liquor in his car, he not only is liable for as much fine and jail sentences as is the drunken driver, but the state can and usually does confiscate and sell his car. The money derived from such car sales goes to the school funds. The result is that Kansans immediately drink their liquor or carefully hide it, but not in their cars.

Considering all this, imagine my surprise a few days before Christmas a year ago when I walked into Mr. White's office and saw a sealed carton on the top of his desk.

"For the love of Mike, what have you got here?" I asked, picking up the box and finding it contained a pint of excellent whiskey.

"I don't know," replied Mr. White, as I handed it to him. "What is it?" He read the label and turned whiter than I ever had seen him before, even the day several years ago when his heart went back on him and he almost fainted while at work.

"Well, you got one on me," he exclaimed. "When I walked into the office just now a salesman handed me the box and said, 'Here's your Christmas present.' I didn't even look at it. Just thanked him and brought it in here. Now what shall I ever do with that?"

"If you can't think of anything better," I suggested, "you might hide it in your desk drawer, take it home, and let Mrs. White mix it up in a batch of mincemeat.

167

The alcohol would all bake out of it and the pies certainly wouldn't be any worse for it."

With that I walked out because I did not want to know what he did with it. But a week later I was a dinner guest at his home and I never tasted better pie.

Even though beer now is legal in Kansas and many papers take beer advertising, the *Gazette* does not.

"I can't afford to," Mr. White says. "I supported the legalizing of beer merely because I felt it would cut down on the hard and more harmful liquor consumed. If I took beer advertising, people would say that was why I favored the legalizing of beer. And even though it is legal, I do not want to advocate its use by taking its advertising."

Mr. White never has smoked and for many years there was an unwritten law prohibiting smoking in the office by *Gazette* employees. The printers and pressmen in the shop smoked anything they wanted and Walter Hughes, for many years business manager, smoked cigars and a pipe in the front office, but no one else smoked anything in the business or editorial offices. When the Whites' son, W. L. White, came home from Harvard in 1924, he smoked where he pleased and others began smoking in the office. Nothing was ever said about it. Although the smoking of cigarettes was legal in Kansas, the sale or free distribution of them was prohibited by state law for many years. After the repeal of the anticigarette law, the tobacco companies flooded Kansas with cigarette advertising, but it was a long time before Mr. White would permit cigarette advertisements in the *Gazette*. He weakened only at the constant urging of everyone else in the office, who pointed out that about every other paper in the state was taking the business.

The first woman I ever saw smoke in the *Gazette* office was in the nineteen twenties when Edna Ferber came to visit the Whites and used a typewriter in our editorial office to write a letter. I watched to see what Mr. White would do, but he never appeared while she was smoking. Since then smoking by women has become common, and the *Gazette* even maintains a lounge room in the basement where women employees smoke.

CHAPTER XVI

FOR FREE SPEECH

EVER SINCE HE HAS EDITED A NEWSPAper, Mr. White has carried the banner for freedom of speech. His fight for that right of man at one time led him into battle against the ruling of another social reform which he had helped establish. The *Gazette* had for years favored an industrial court where disputes between employers and employees could be heard. Finally the Kansas Industrial Court was set up. Henry Allen, Wichita editor, who later became a United States senator and who for many years has been a close personal and political friend of Mr. White, was Governor of Kansas when the railway shopmen struck in 1922.

During the strike the idle shopworkers passed out to those of their friends who would accept them window cards which read: "We are for the striking railroad men 100 per cent. We are for a living wage and fair working conditions." Many of the cards were

170

placed in display windows of stores and shops and immediately the Industrial Court ordered them out. Upon hearing of the order, Mr. White immediately sent for one of the cards, crossed out the "100 per cent," made it read "49 per cent," and placed the card in a *Gazette* window.

"The court order is an infamous infraction of the right of the free press and free speech," Mr. White wrote in an editorial the same day. "Certainly it has not come to such a pass in this country that a man may not say what he thinks about an industrial controversy without disobeying the law. One of these cards went up in the *Gazette* window today. Instead of 100 per cent, we have started it at 49 per cent. If the strike lasts until tomorrow we shall change the percentage to 50, and move it up a little every day. As a matter of fact, the *Gazette* does not believe that anyone—not even the *Gazette*—is 100 per cent right. But somewhere between 49 and 100 per cent the men are right. And if the Industrial Court desires to make a test case, here it is. This is not a question of whether the men are right or wrong, but the question of an American citizen's right to say what he pleases about this strike. And if 49 per cent sympathy is permissible, in the next fifty days we shall see where violation of

171

the law begins. The Industrial Court, which we have upheld since its inception, and still uphold, will have the nicest little chance to see just where it is lawful for a man to express his sympathy with his friends and neighbors, even if in his heart he believes that they have made a mistake in the time of their strike. Either we have free speech and a free press in this country or we have not. Now is the time to find out."

News of Mr. White's defiance of the Industrial Court order prohibiting the display of signs favoring the strikers was sent out to newspapers and press associations. The next day Mr. White was ordered arrested by his old friend and fellow editor, Governor Allen, and the Emporian went to the courthouse and signed bond for his freedom pending a trial which never came. Mr. White repeatedly urged the state to take him to trial, but the matter dragged on. Other newspapers and the general public rallied more to the cause of the strikers because of the court's attitude in the White case, but despite that the shopmen lost their strike. Finally the suit against Mr. White was dismissed, against his protest, and later the Industrial Court passed out of the picture.

All during the free-speech fight between Mr. White and the court, the Whites and the Allens remained close friends and visited each other's homes. Many persons thought for this reason that the whole thing was a publicity scheme, but it was merely two friends fighting for something in which they believed, but both big enough not to let their differences interfere with their friendship. Only once during the whole affair did I hear the two men argue privately over the question and that time Mrs. White stopped it.

"Now see here, you two," she said, smiling. "This is a social visit and remember we are not going to discuss your differences."

Everyone laughed and neither the strike, the Industrial Court, nor free speech was mentioned during the remainder of the visit.

Mr. White did win an unusual honor during the controversy. For an editorial he wrote as an open letter to Governor Allen, he won a Pulitzer prize as the best editorial of 1922. Headed "To an Anxious Friend," the editorial follows:

"You tell me that law is above freedom of utterance. And I reply that you can have no wise laws nor free enforcement of wise laws unless there is free expression of the wisdom of the people—and, alas, their folly with it. But if there is freedom, folly will die of its own poison, and the wisdom will survive. That is the

173

history of the race. It is the proof of man's kinship with God. You say that freedom of utterance is not for time of stress, and I reply with the sad truth that only in time of stress is freedom of utterance in danger. No one questions it in calm days, because it is not needed. And the reverse is true also; only when free utterance is suppressed is it needed, and when it is needed, it is most vital to justice. Peace is good. But if you are interested in peace through force and without free discussion, that is to say, free utterance decently and in order—your interest in justice is slight. And peace without justice is tyranny, no matter how you may sugar-coat it with expediency. This state today is in more danger from suppression than from violence, because in the end suppression leads to violence. Violence, indeed, is the child of suppression. Whoever pleads for justice helps to keep the peace; and whoever tramples upon the plea for justice, temperately made in the name of peace, only outrages peace and kills something fine in the heart of man which God put there when we got our manhood. When that is killed, brute meets brute on each side of the line.

"So, dear friend, put fear out of your heart. This nation will survive, this state will prosper, the orderly business of life will go forward if only men can speak in whatever way given them to utter what their hearts hold—by voice, by posted card, by letter, or by press. Reason never has failed men. Only force and repression have made the wrecks in the world."

Labor troubles have never bothered the *Gazette*. At one time the men in the mechanical department were affiliated with the printers' union, but the office workers never have belonged to the guild. After years of membership in the printers' union, the mechanical men voted to surrender their charter in the early nineteen twenties. "We didn't have any reason to have a union," one of the old-timers explained to me recently. "We had no fight with the boss, our working conditions were good, and we just decided to give up the union."

About six months after the union had been abandoned, one of the men walked into Mr. White's office and asked if he could get a raise. He was thinking of getting married.

"Where's your grievance committee?" asked Mr. White.

"Our what!" exclaimed the workman. "Didn't you know we gave up our charter a long time ago?"

It was the first news Mr. White had had of it. The man received a raise.

When the present Federal Wage and Hour Law was passed, Mr. White announced firmly that the law was to be followed to the letter. All *Gazette* employees already were getting higher wages than the minimum provided by law and were working short weeks. For years the *Gazette* had been publishing two editions each weekday except Saturday and only one, at noon, on Saturday. That gave the employees from Saturday noon until Monday morning to do as they pleased. Most of the employees did not want to work less time and some suggested ways in which the *Gazette* might get around the new law. Other publishers told Mr. White of ways of wage readjustment which would permit the men to work the same number of hours at the same pay or less.

"We are not going to try to get around the law," Mr. White declared. "While there are some parts of it we do not like, it is a step in the right direction and we are not going to try to evade it or defy it. We'll comply in every way and we'll come out of it some way."

As one of the men charged with seeing that the law is obeyed, I know that there are no willful violations. The hardest part of the enforcement is getting the reporters to confine their work to forty hours a week.

176

If they are not watched carefully, they fudge and work more than their allotted time each week and think nothing of it. The big job is to make the workers stick to the law. The real reason behind the reaction of the *Gazette* employees is that for many years Mr. White has been giving his workers the things that many workers over the country did not get until the government stepped in and regulated wages and hours.

CHAPTER XVII

THE BANNER OF PEACE

M R. WHITE, LIKE OTHERS IN THE
Middle West and West, was slow to become
wrought up over the First World War. Not until the
sinking of the "Lusitania" did he feel it was in any
sense a war in which the United States had any chips,
and even then he did not become emotional in his editorials. Until that time, Mr. White believed that the
European struggle was none of our affair and even
afterward, in an editorial, he warned this country not
to become war mad as was most of the rest of the
world. Even the attack on the American ship "Gul-
flight" and the death of two Americans did not stir
him to the point of wanting to become involved in the
war. While he had a feeling of contempt for Germany
following the rape of Belgium and the attacks on ships,
his attitude toward England was not cordial and he
condemned Great Britain's policy of commercialism
which shielded shipments of arms and munitions by

carrying passengers on the same boats with war goods.

"But neither German barbarism nor English Philistinism furnishes us an excuse as Americans for running amuck when all the world is mad," Mr. White wrote in an editorial on May 10, 1915. "Some high devil in the forces of hell seems to have found a lever that has turned into the streets all the madness of humanity that is pent up in human hearts. The world's highways are filled with homicides. Let all sane men go in and shut their doors. To go out means contagion and death. Americans—South Americans and North Americans—hold the ark of the covenant of civilization. In a world gone mad, we have the peace that passeth understanding. By God's grace we should keep it."

Germany's submarine warfare on neutral vessels finally changed the Emporian, and nearly a month before the United States actually declared war on Germany, Mr. White wrote that "We have been in war for two years. When the 'Lusitania' went down, after its destruction was advertised in the newspapers, war on America and American rights was declared by the German princes. But we have been long-suffering. We have turned the other cheek until it is calloused with blows. We need no longer wait for further provocation. We are at war. And being at war, we should defend ourselves. We should open the seas to American commerce."

All through the First World War Mr. White preached in his editorial column that this war was against a militaristic German government and not against the German people. It was highly improbable, he felt, that hatred against the Germans would exist for generations, as some people believed, and he predicted that Germany would be "received back into the companionship of the nations" after the war because Germany would "come back a new Germany, with a government typical of the kindly German people and not the party which, in the midst of civilization, has inflicted upon the world more horror and more atrocity than it has known for centuries."

Hardly had the First World War ended before Mr. White was telling his readers that it had not solved anything and that the peoples of the earth were confronted with more problems than ever before. As an observer for the American Red Cross, he had gone to Europe with Henry Allen, publisher of the *Wichita Beacon,* in 1917, to study the work the Red Cross was doing. There he observed general conditions in the nations that had been at war. As a reporter for an

180

American newspaper syndicate at the Peace Conference in Paris, he saw the leaders of nations battling for
places at the pole in the race for recovery.

"The real job of the Peace Conference," he wrote
in a dispatch dated from Paris on Feb. 19, 1919,
"now that a tentative draft of the League of Nations
has set that top spinning, is to find some way to let go
of the tail of the bear; Germany being the bear, and
her tremendous economic advantage being the unde-
sirable tail. As it stands, Germany, the vanquished, has
the economic advantage over France, the victor. No
matter how high the bill of damages may be, there still
remains a German advantage in the situation which
damages will not remove. . . . In France the white
scar of ruins stretches like a leprous scale from the
mountains to the sea. Cities are wrecked, farms are
bombed into waste land, commerce is blighted, homes
are ruined, civilization is blanched and dead. The
blighted area is from fifty to seventy-five miles wide.
Then it stops sharply as if some terrific fire had been
checked and at the German border we see another
picture. There the cities are untouched, the farms fat
and smiling, business is proceeding as usual, homes
are comfortable and civilization functioning as though
no great war had touched it. Furnace fires are glowing

181

in the factories and, while raw materials are lacking and most factories are working only half time, yet upon the whole the complicated thing called life is proceeding throughout Germany without serious impediment. . . . When the amount of the bill for damages is rendered, Germany will pay it. . . . Germany will start in the race for the world's markets abreast with England and ahead of France. She is the irony of the victory for which we fought. It is tragically unfair, and of course the Peace Conference will not let this condition rest. But how to change this condition, how to take from Germany her economic advantage, how to let go of the tail of this bear, is a puzzling question."

Observing at first hand the sorry mess of war and the difficulties of men trying to arrange a fair and satisfactory peace at the close of war, and himself a lifelong advocate of peace although he did succumb to what he thought was the justice of America's entry in the First World War, it was only natural that the Emporian should join in the work for the League of Nations, the World Court, and other movements he hoped would abolish war. And as these movements failed, Mr. White lamented the fact editorially in the *Gazette*.

The Japanese-China war, the Spanish war, and the Italian invasion of Ethiopia were watched with inter-

182

est by Mr. White, but he did not become alarmed in fear of a general war. Only when Hitler repudiated the terms of the treaty ending the First World War did the Emporian begin to fear a general outbreak. Germany's invasion of Poland and of Czechoslovakia, Russia's conquering of Finland, the Italian-German and Russian-German alliances did worry him tremendously, and all through these events he came from his office into the newsroom of the *Gazette* every hour or so to read the news as it came over the Associated Press printers and to check the happenings with the telegraph editor. He did not see how England and France could keep out of it, yet he worried in fear of what might happen if they got in. Mrs. White worried along with him and showed a keen interest in the happenings, calling the office from her home at intervals during the days to learn the latest developments.

Why, some people asked, should Mr. White show so much interest and worry so much over this war when he had felt for several years of the First World War that it was a foreign affair and the United States should keep out? The German war lords of the first war had announced no world scheme and had said nothing of a far future when "mankind may face problems which can be surmounted only by a supreme

183

master race supported by means and resources of the entire group." There were spies in the old war, but the fifth column was unheard of and Germany at that time had made no such propaganda and educational invasion of South America and Mexico as had been done under the Nazi regime. War machines had been improved, especially in Germany. Other countries, particularly the United States, had not kept pace. These were the things that worried Mr. White as the present war progressed.

"Not only is the United States vulnerable, but just consider Kansas and Emporia," he told us in the office one day when we were watching the news come in over the telegraph wires. "If Hitler should conquer Europe, it would be easy for him to get a good hold in this hemisphere, and if he got control in Mexico, where would he attack the United States if he wanted to take us on? With the British navy out of the way, of course the eastern seaboard would be open, for we have no Atlantic fleet, but think of what else might happen! Emporia is only a few hours from Mexico by airplane. Fort Riley (seventy miles northwest of Emporia and the geographical center of the United States) is our biggest cavalry school and one of our strong

184

military posts, and just think how close it is by war-
plane to the Mexican border!"

We who knew Mr. White well remembered how
slow he was to become excited over the First World
War; we knew how he believed in fighting only as a
last resort. Even in ordinary things which came up
around the newspaper, he would go to almost any
limit to avoid a row. Knowing that any kind of trouble
worried him to the extent that he took those worries
home with him at night and kept them in his mind
all the time, we were not surprised when he took the
lead to aid Great Britain in hopes of keeping the
United States out of war.

Mr. White's adventure with the Committee to Defend America by Aiding the Allies was little different
from his campaign to keep the Emporia Y.M.C.A. going, his work to help organize a local community chest
campaign, or his efforts to bring the Kansas City Sym-
phony Orchestra to Emporia once a year for concerts.
He did not get into the committee to aid the allies
merely because someone asked him to, because not a
day passes but that he is asked to serve on this committee or that, to be an active or honorary officer of
some organization, or to lend his name to a board or
campaign formed for some purpose or other. He be-

came interested in the work of aiding the allies because he felt it was the thing Americans should do. Always he has been an advocate of peace, but if necessary he is willing to fight to keep peace.

In the case of aiding the allies against Germany, Mr. White has not believed and does not now believe that the United States should send men to Europe to fight Hitler, because he does not believe that England needs our men. But he does believe the United States is in danger if England is defeated, and he believes that the United States should do its part to defend democracy and the United States by sending all the help it can to Europe as soon as possible, excepting men, who should go only as a last resort.

Mr. White has been prominent nationally in advocating peace since thirty-five years ago when he became a director of the League to Enforce Peace, an organization formed by William Howard Taft, Elihu Root, Charles Evans Hughes, and others. Before the First World War, this group worked hard to make their organization popular in this country and to set up similar organizations in Europe, Mexico, and South America. In this group, which financially was supported largely by Andrew Carnegie, the Emporia editor gained the fundamentals of his attitude toward international affairs.

As an American newspaper syndicate reporter in Paris covering the Peace Conference after the First World War, he felt the injustices of the peace treaty. He supported the League of Nations and he urged the United States to join. He paid his own expenses and made his own dates for speaking engagements to plead for the league. Likewise he supported a world court, doing everything he could as an editor and an individual to help movements he thought would make a better understanding between nations of the world.

So in the fall of 1939 when Clark Eichelberger, who had been secretary of the League of Nations Association, telephoned and then came to Emporia to ask Mr. White to be chairman of a committee to work for repeal of this country's embargo act, it was only natural that Mr. White should accept. The embargo act prohibited the sale for shipment from the United States of guns, fighting planes, and other completed implements of war, but it did permit the United States not only to sell but also to ship in American boats materials from which these same implements of war could be made. The organizers of the proposed committee felt—and it was something Mr. White had felt for

187

many years—that the embargo act would get the United States into the war quicker than any other thing and for that reason he accepted the committee's chairmanship just as he led the fight in Kansas against the Ku Klux Klan in the early nineteen twenties.

If the United States continued to ship in American boats all kinds of materials for making war machines and contraband of war to the fighting nations, Mr. White believed sincerely that Germany would sink American boats and the United States again would be at war, just as we got into the First World War, when President Wilson tried to maintain the freedom of the seas and the attacks on the American vessels caused our declaration of war on Germany.

But before joining the men and women who were forming the committee to work for the repeal of the embargo act, the Emporian first satisfied himself that it was an organization of sincere, peace-loving Americans such as he and that capitalists interested mainly in selling war goods to Europe were not involved. Satisfying himself on that issue, he not only agreed to take the committee's chairmanship, but he began putting all his efforts into the work. While others looked after the details of the committee, Mr. White held the reins of its policy with a firm hand, and he had only one thing in mind—to help the peaceful nations of the world against the belligerents. The Emporian took no part in the committee's money-raising campaign, which was left to a professional organization which was paid for its work. He wrote editorials which appeared in the *Gazette* and then went over the country to be published in newspapers as statements of the committee in its effort to gain public support for the repeal of the embargo.

The committee, which meant Mr. White, because he kept his hand on the policies, naturally got into politics as it worked for the repeal of the embargo act, and it worked to make sure that neither major political party before the 1940 election had in its platform a plank which would be against aid to Great Britain. In this work the committee played no favorites, and Mr. White was on the telephone talking to President Roosevelt—who controlled the Democratic party platform and its campaign—as often as he was talking with Wendell Willkie and other Republican leaders concerning that party's affairs. Working close to him all during this time, I could not help but hear much of what he said and to whom he was speaking.

This effort of Mr. White and the committee to play fair and aboveboard with both parties was the one

189

thing that got the Emporian into a jam with the Republicans in his own community and state. As I said before, most of the official statements of the Committee to Defend America by Aiding the Allies first appeared as editorials in the *Gazette,* and naturally in those statements Mr. White gave Roosevelt and the Democrats credit for things they did which were in line with the committee's work. Every time one of these statements appeared, local Republicans began "jumping" members of the *Gazette* staff because they thought Mr. White was supporting the Democrats. We in the office understood and tried to defend the boss's work with the committee and explain why he had to give credit to both sides alike when they favored the committee, but it was a struggle. Many times I took editorials Mr. White had written back to his office and asked him to write another paragraph explaining that he still felt Wendell Willkie was the man for president, even though both candidates seemed to see eye to eye on the European situation. Sometimes he added these paragraphs to his editorials, but never without an argument that he could not see why people did not realize he was for Willkie even if he did give Roosevelt some credit.

All during the work of the committee—which included the disposal of old United States destroyers to Great Britain and the sale of bombers—Mr. White worked more for the committee than he did for himself and his paper. Long-distance telephone calls came into the *Gazette* office all day long, and local affairs, usually his first interest, got little of Mr. White's attention while he conferred with bigwigs in the departments of state, army and navy, the President, and many others. The College of Emporia, which for many years had been Mr. White's personal pet and a "sacred cow" of the *Gazette,* was going through its worst financial crisis and Mr. White paid little attention, so busy was he with his committee. All the department heads in the *Gazette* office had lists of things which had to be settled and on which they wanted his advice. Many things had been done which would not have been done in ordinary times without the consultation and advice of the boss.

CHAPTER XVIII

THE ALLIED COMMITTEE

ALL THIS TIME HE WAS WEARING HIM-self down and down. Nearly seventy-three years old, he could not stand the strain of all the work. Mrs. White worried about him until she became ill and her doctor ordered her to the Southwest for a rest. Many times I heard Mr. White's physician, who has his office on the second floor of the *Gazette* building, warn the editor that "You're going to kill yourself if you don't lay off this stuff and let some younger man do it."

So for those reasons, it was no surprise to the *Gazette* force when in early January Mr. White resigned as chairman of the Committee to Defend America by Aiding the Allies. Early in November he had said he would like to resign from the committee chairmanship so he could settle down again as just a country editor, but vital questions were involved and he did not want to quit while the battle was on. While he was in New York in November, I went to Louisville,

"I know this was taken in 1918 because I'll never forget that suit," said the Editor. "Good material was scarce then. Look at the way that baby hangs!"

Ky., to a meeting of the Associated Press Managing Editors' Association. There I found Barry Bingham and Neil Dalton, of the *Louisville Courier-Journal*, had scheduled a big meeting of the Committee to Defend America by Aiding the Allies. They had tried to get Mr. White to come to Louisville for the meeting, but he had said it was impossible. They suggested that I ask him again, so I called him and wrote him a letter. Again he explained that he could not and on Nov. 22 he wrote me:

"I just couldn't go to the Louisville meeting. I was tied up with things here in New York that were of considerable importance. We expect to be home about the first. We will be leaving here the 28th for Washington for two or three days. I am having a busy time. Every hour seems to be scheduled. This committee job is both getting my goat and renewing my youth. When you get to be in your seventies, you'll know what I mean."

I lack a lot of being in my seventies, but I know what he meant. Mr. White was tired and worn. He wanted to quit it all and come home to edit his newspaper and rest. But he retained enough of his spirit of youth that he did not want to quit until the job was done.

As Emporia's 150 Kansas National Guardsmen were mobilized during the Christmas holidays before going to Camp Robinson, Ark., for a year of training, Mr. White watched with interest and many times I heard him say that he hoped they never would have to fight on our soil or abroad and that during the present war he would never be for sending them abroad so long as Great Britain had a chance of winning with her own men and machines and the help, excepting men, we could give England.

But tomorrow, if he should decide England needed men, he could change as quickly as he could change from his pajamas to his street clothes and hurry to the *Gazette* office to write an editorial on the need of sending men to Europe. But he would have to be satisfied in his own mind that England needed men. Last winter a telephone call from his son, who was in London writing about the war, failed to change the Emporia editor. The son maintained England needed men, but the father disagreed. He not only said so over the telephone, but he wrote a short piece for the first page of the *Gazette* telling of the call and reiterating his own opinion that England had the man power if she could only get the machines.

Late in the summer of 1940, when the presidential

194

campaign was going strong and Mr. White, as chairman of the Committee to Defend America by Aiding the Allies, was working hard with both parties for his committee, Mr. and Mrs. White decided they needed a vacation in Colorado. Picking up a driver for their car and a maid to take care of their two cabins near Estes Park, they started for the mountains, stopping on the way at Colorado Springs to see Wendell Willkie, who was spending a few days there. Their cabins had been put in readiness before they arrived—the water turned on, beds put in order, and the telephone connected. Any urgent business of the defense committee, Mr. White knew, could be taken care of by long distance telephone.

There was nothing secret about the committee's work. Mr. White was in close touch with leaders of both parties, trying hard to keep them lined up for aid to Britain and a strong defense program for the United States. The Whites knew there would be many telephone calls and they planned that Mrs. White would keep the driver of the car away from the main cabin and the maid busy in another room when Mr. White was on the telephone. They had everything planned and when the telephone rang—Washington calling— just as they arrived at their mountain retreat, Mr.

195

White went to the telephone and Mrs. White went into action, getting the others away so that Mr. White could talk in quiet.

For a couple of weeks everything went well. They rested on the big porch at the front of their main cabin, they drove in the mountains, and evenings they read in front of the roaring blaze in the big fireplace. Despite the many telephone calls to and from New York, Washington, and many other cities where the defense committee and government officials and party leaders were, the Whites were getting the rest they much needed. Mr. White had made no public appearances, except to attend a couple of meetings of the local Rotary Club, so when a group from the local chapter of the Committee to Defend America by Aiding the Allies asked him to speak at their next meeting, he consented.

"Today we are to hear from a very busy and very prominent man," said the presiding officer, addressing the large crowd. "Although he is here for a vacation and a rest, which he greatly deserves, this man has not been idle."

Mr. and Mrs. White looked at each other, each feeling rather smug at the realization of how busy Mr.

196

White actually had been while he was supposed to be just resting in the mountains.

"Although he has been hundreds—even thousands— of miles from the busy offices of his committee and our government," the chairman continued, "this man has not forsaken his duty. He has been in almost constant touch with the New York office of the Committee to Defend America by Aiding the Allies."

Mr. and Mrs. White again looked at each other, each with a look of "Who's been telling this man things?"

"More than that," continued the chairman, "this man has talked many times with high government officials in Washington. Not only has he talked with the secretary of war and the secretary of the navy, but he has been called by the President of the United States. It is my pleasure to present William Allen White."

By that time both Mr. and Mrs. White had turned a pea-green color and all during Mr. White's speech they wondered who had told what was going on in the cabin. Each knew the other had not told and immediately after the program they rushed to the chairman.

"How in the world," asked Mr. White, "did you find out about my telephone calls? Who could have known about them and told?"

197

"Oh, that's no secret," replied the chairman. "Everybody in Estes Park knows all about what's been going on. Didn't you know that your telephone was on a party line? Every time your telephone rings the people in half a dozen other houses take down their receivers and listen to the conversation."

CHAPTER XIX

DON'T MENTION THE BOSS

MR. WHITE HAS A STREAK OF MODESTY
—perhaps it is temperament—which caused
him to make and for years enforce a rule which prohibited the use of his name in the *Gazette* except when
he gave specific permission. As a result, Emporians
who were *Gazette* readers often knew less of his activities than did people in other cities and towns. For
example, when he made addresses in the East, his
speeches generally were reported in metropolitan papers and carried over the wires of the press associations. When they came into the *Gazette* office over the
Associated Press, they were read by the men in the
newsroom and then left on Mr. White's desk for him
to see or were thrown into a wastebasket. Often the
speeches, which were written before he left Emporia,
had been printed in part as editorials in the *Gazette*.
But generally speaking, the rest of the world read
more of Mr. White's public life than did Emporians.

199

Gradually the rule has changed and in recent years we have slipped more and more things about him into the paper without asking him. It started by running stories about him when he was out of town and gradually he has broken down and let us print more about him when he is in town, but such items must be of enough importance that they appear on the reports of the press associations. In the year and a half of his work with the committee to aid the allies, the *Gazette* printed more news of Mr. White than it had printed about him in any other ten years of his activities.

But these infractions of his "no self-publicity rule" have been only when he appeared in the national picture. His ordinary activities still get little publicity in the *Gazette,* except when he writes a travelogue editorial after he has taken a trip. Emporians look forward to these pieces when they know Mr. White has been away, and when he returns and fails to write one, he receives many complaints. But still more than half of his trips rate only two- or three-line items in the *Gazette.*

The rule is a tough one on conventions which come to Emporia. At nearly every convention, the editor is asked to be a speaker and frequently he does appear on the program. When the convention is reported by the *Gazette,* the boss's speech is ignored, except to bury in the middle of some paragraph the two letters and two words, "W. A. White spoke." Frequently the heads of the convention come to the *Gazette* to protest that the programs were not adequately covered by *Gazette* reporters, and when you pin them down they always refer to Mr. White's speech. When the rule is explained, they usually go away baffled. Some get angry.

The Emporia editor has a knack of making things he writes serve more than one purpose. Often when he writes a letter to someone, dealing with some phase of public life, he will have an extra carbon copy made and with a few words for an introduction and possibly a "kicker" on the end, he will use much of the letter as the body of an editorial. A long speech, prepared for some school or organization, frequently serves to make several editorials. Sometimes he makes the same speech serve for different audiences, as for example in 1935 when he gave the commencement address at Harvard University. A week before the program at Cambridge, I drove him to Admire, a small town about twenty miles from Emporia, in the *Gazette's* trade territory, where he gave part of the Harvard address before a high school graduating class of less than a dozen.

201

Usually Mr. White gives one major commencement address each spring, always turning down many more invitations to speak. He likes to give one each year, if he has time, at some large school, but he would rather speak at the smaller towns in Emporia's territory, from which *Gazette* advertisers get their business. It is not as mercenary as it sounds, however, for the Emporia editor likes to be with the people of the district he serves, and for that reason he tries to attend as many of their fairs and community celebrations as he can.

Mr. White always is good for a talk at the Rotary Club and never has failed to respond when asked. He also talks many times during the year to other men's service clubs, church groups, women's organizations, and public meetings in and near Emporia. Early in the summer of 1940, after he had returned from a few weeks in New York and Washington, Mr. White was asked by the Rotary Club to give the weekly program, telling what he heard in the East about the European war. Totally ignoring his subject, he talked for half an hour on Wendell Willkie. Mr. White realized that the Emporians knew little about Willkie and the editor had been with Willkie several times on his Eastern trip, twice introducing at dinner meetings the man who was later to become the Republican presidential nominee. Mr. White knew that it was more important at that time for the Rotarians to learn something of Willkie, and later, as Willkie came more and more into the limelight, the Rotarians saw why Mr. White had changed his subject and they were glad of it.

Although Mr. White likes modern things such as automobiles and radios, he likes them only if he can enjoy them without having to operate them. He has never learned to drive a car and he has no patience at all with a radio. The Whites have owned automobiles since the early nineteen hundreds and Mr. White tried to drive only once. That time he went about a block, stopped against a telephone pole, and has not been in the driver's seat since. Mrs. White drives him about town when it is possible for her to do so. She arranges her household work to suit his plans and she even leaves parties and meetings early so she can take him home from the office.

Their son, Bill, did most of the driving when he was a boy and until he grew up, had his own car, and finally was married and moved to his own home. Their daughter, Mary, was an excellent driver even as a youngster. When she was in high school, until her death, she drove her parents many places. In recent years Mrs. White has done most of the driving in town, with the housekeeper, Miss Bertha Colglazier, filling in when Mrs. White was not available. The men in the *Gazette* office volunteer to take the boss home when they can get away from their work, and frequently he lets them do it. Many times he lingers in the office making preparations to go home and sometimes he announces he is ready to go, but never have I heard him come right out and ask anyone in the office to take him. If the family car is not available with a driver and no one volunteers to take him, he walks or calls a taxi. But he uses taxis only if the weather is extremely bad. When there were several unmarried men in the office, they frequently were asked to drive the Whites on trips, because Mrs. White never drives out of town. I have driven the Whites all over Kansas in all kinds of weather, before the roads were paved and when mud driving was common. Never once have I heard them complain of the driving, except to say that forty-five miles an hour was fast enough. They do not like speed, but nothing else bothers them. Coming home from a trip to Wichita one time we got caught in the rain with seventy-five miles of dirt road before us. Three times we went into ditches and twice had to get farmers to pull us out.

Finally arriving at Eureka, still more than forty miles from home, Mr. White announced:

"You're a good driver, but I've had enough mud. We will stay here tonight."

After a movie, a good sleep, and breakfast at a hotel, we started on again and three and a half hours later we arrived at Madison, still twenty miles from Emporia. There Mr. and Mrs. White announced they had to attend a funeral that afternoon and they thought they would take the train, which was about due. A half hour later they were in Emporia. I pulled in four hours later, after stopping dozens of times to dig the heavy, rolling mud from between the wheels and the fenders and finally giving two farm boys five dollars to pull me with a team the last four miles to the Emporia paved streets. After putting the car in a garage for a general cleaning, I decided to check up on the Whites. They really had gone to a funeral.

Knowing nothing about the handling of a motorcar, Mr. White does not like the new models and if he could get good cars in old styles he would buy them. He owned an old touring car for many years after sedans were on the market, but he did not mind. About 1926 he bought a secondhand coach—made for three people but which would carry four—and he loved it because it was high in the air and because he could see out over the landscape while someone else drove. The fact that newer cars were safer and were easier to handle did not bother him, and not until he was in a friend's car, which overturned and slid on its steel top, did he finally give in and admit that one car was safer than another. The old coach had brakes on only the rear wheels and was hard to handle in traffic, which was thick with newer models. We in the office tried for years to get him to buy a new car, but he thought the old one was good enough, and even Mrs. White, who did the town driving, argued that there was no sense in spending a lot of money for a new car. Finally, when the coach had been driven so much that he could not deny repair bills were amounting to about as much as the car was worth, a dealer came along with a three-year-old sedan—a high model with lots of glass windows. This the Whites used for trips for about ten years, finally trading it in on a new 1938 powerful sedan. In the meantime they had traded the old coach in on a new coupé for Mrs. White to drive in town. The two-year-old sedan still serves them, and to show how little Mr. White knows about the modern motorcar, here is what he told me as he rode home with me in a two-year-old flivver.

206

"That sedan of ours," he said, "is a fine car. You know we have had it two years and it has made two trips to Colorado and back and hasn't given us a bit of trouble." Colorado is only about five hundred miles away.

Mr. White is not superstitious and to prove it his cars always carry license numbers 13-1300 and 13-1313. The first number, 13, is the one assigned to all cars in Lyon County. The 1300 and 1313 he gets by telling the county treasurer, who issues the tags, that he wants them. He tells her the first day the tags go on sale and she calls the *Gazette* the day his numbers come up.

Although Mr. and Mrs. White have two radios in their home, they seldom listen to them. Both are mantel sets, a small one in bookshelves in the living room and a larger one on a table in Mr. White's up-stairs study. Except when their son, Bill, was broad-casting from Europe in the winter of 1939-1940 for the Columbia Broadcasting System, the Whites never have listened regularly to the radio. During this time, however, nothing could keep them away from the radio during the fifteen minutes their son talked every evening. Several times while Bill was in Finland his father and mother arranged dinner parties with Bill's friends as guests. After listening to the broadcast, Mr.

207

White would place a long distance telephone call and catch Bill at the broadcasting station. Bill's friends would listen attentively while Mr. and Mrs. White talked with their son, and then they would tell the friends everything he said.

Now, except for occasional news broadcasts and special events such as addresses by President Roosevelt or other prominent men, the Whites' radios remain silent. During the 1940 political campaign, however, they were attentive listeners to Willkie's speeches.

Although Mr. White's speeches sometimes are broadcast when he is in the East and several years ago the Columbia Broadcasting Company sent Gilbert Seldes from New York and a technical crew from St. Louis to put on a thirty-minute broadcast of the work in the *Gazette* office for Columbia's "Americans at Work" series, radio does not get much house in the *Gazette*. Radio, the *Gazette* believes, is more than anything else a competitor of the newspaper and for that reason the *Gazette* prints no radio programs. Except for important, unsponsored programs, such as addresses by the President, radio gets no free announcements in the *Gazette*. A small radio station is operated in Emporia and is treated by the *Gazette* as is any other business. It has to make news to get into print without buying

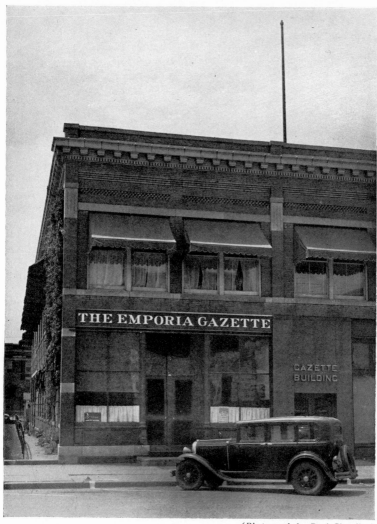

(*Photograph by Paul Chandler.*)

The Whites Love This Old-fashioned Front of the *Gazette* Building. The Newspaper Uses the First Floor and Basement.

advertising. Its programs are not mentioned. Neither does the *Gazette* ask or expect anything from the radio.

Mr. White was reluctant to accept the radio from the first. The White family was one of the last in town to buy one. When sets first began to come out with loud-speakers in cabinets, a large manufacturer of the new sets wrote Mr. White, asking him if he would accept one as a gift. Because he does not like anyone to give him anything of any great monetary value and because he knew the company might want to use his name in advertising, he declined the offer. Another letter came from the manufacturer, citing the wonders of radio and ending with a suggestion that the Emporia editor would enjoy listening to President Coolidge's broadcasts. Again Mr. White declined, answering the Coolidge suggestion with the statement that he could always read the President's speeches and "besides, we have a good electric refrigerator." Not until several years later did the Whites buy a radio.

CHAPTER XX

AROUND THE OFFICE

MR. WHITE'S REFUSAL TO ACCEPT THE radio as a gift is true to his trait of wanting to pay for what he gets and his willingness to pay a fair price. He appreciates good service and for that, too, he expects to pay. Tipping is not generally done in small towns such as Emporia, but I have never seen Mr. White leave a table in a café without leaving something for the waiter or waitress. And if he gets caught without any money, which frequently happens, he borrows enough from someone to leave a tip and then he signs the check. Never does he fail to pay back what he borrows, although he sometimes forgets it for a while.

Last October, on a day when he was leaving for New York, we were having luncheon at an Emporia hotel with a group of farmers and cattlemen, all guests of Mr. White. After the meal he asked me to lend him a dollar to tip the waitress and he signed the check.

When we returned to the office, several persons were waiting to see him and I did not talk with him again until he returned from the East several weeks later. In January—three months later—a group of us were eating in another café, and as we left Mr. White pulled several dollar bills from his pocket, left one on the table for the waitress, and handed me another.

"Here," he said, "is that dollar I borrowed from you last fall to pay the waitress at the Broadview."

"Oh—that—well—" I replied, "I drew that from the cash register and charged it to your account when we got back to the office that day."

"Good for you," he exclaimed. "That's what you should have done. Remind me some day to take you out of the editorial room and put you in the collection department."

It is the same way when he borrows a pencil from a desk. Ordinarily he uses his big red pen for everything, but occasionally he picks up a pencil and goes to some other desk to work. But he never fails to return it, although the *Gazette* buys all the pencils used in the office. One day before he and Mrs. White were leaving for Europe, he took a new pencil from my desk, signed for a telegram which had just been delivered to him, and stuck the pencil in his pocket.

Months later, a few days after he had returned from his trip, he walked in and dropped a stub of a yellow pencil on my desk with the mere remark:

"Here's that pencil I borrowed the day I went away."

When Mr. White goes to New York—and he usually goes four to six times a year, taking Mrs. White with him when she can go—he sees all the new plays he can. Then when the shows come to Emporia several years later, as road shows, he goes again. Motion pictures entertain him and he has said many times that all shows are good, although some are better than others. Modern drama and sophisticated comedies please him and occasionally he goes to a historical "heavy," but the slapstick comedies get most of his enthusiasm for the movies. Laurel and Hardy, he says, are his favorites and he has gone to see them in England, France, Italy, China, and Russia.

Mr. White, a rapid reader, skims through many magazines, but he reads few, spending most of his reading time on books and newspapers. With all the entries for the Book of the Month Club he has to read each month as a judge, he has little time for reading other than the newspapers. The *Gazette* receives about fifty newspapers, most of them from Kansas, at its exchange table each day and when Mr. White is at the office he glances through nearly all of them. Through years of reading them, he knows about which ones will furnish him ideas for editorials, which ones will have editorials concerning him or Emporia, and which ones are most likely to have news stories that will give him tips for *Gazette* stories. These news items he clips out with one of the two pocketknives he always carries and he brings them one by one to my desk with suggestions. Of the many papers on the exchange table, I believe Mr. White can pick out at least half of them by glancing at the wrapper and without opening it. The color of the wrapper and a peek at the headline type on the rolled paper are enough to tell him.

Mr. White is not one who minds mixing fun with work and he gets as much kick out of joking around the office as anyone does. Seldom does he walk through the office but he makes a "fast crack" at someone, usually about something new he or she is wearing. He notices new clothes and particularly new hair styles on the women.

Once when I found a half-starved and injured kitten under the front porch at home, probably where a dog had chased it, I took it to the office, which is full of people who like cats. We told Mr. White we wanted to keep it for an office cat and to name it "Copy." John Moore and Sam Gage, the janitors, who were not exactly lovers of cats, did not think much of the idea and when Ted McDaniel, sports editor, and I told the boss of our plan, we suggested that we would appreciate any little help he could give us. In a few minutes, the following typewritten bulletin, signed by Mr. White, appeared on the bulletin board beside the water cooler in the print shop:

"ENLARGING OUR EQUIPMENT

"Mice are overrunning the basement and the second floor of the *Gazette* building, doing considerable damage. I have therefore decided to add to our already extensive equipment one double cylinder T-model repossessed cat. Be good to the cat! Don't let him feed in the melting pot and don't throw slugs at him for walking on the keyboards of the machines. The girls in the front office will feed him. Mr. Moore and Mr. Gage have been engaged to do chamber work for the cat, and all the force will be asked to do is to be kind to him and in an emergency drown part of his kittens.

"W. A. WHITE."

But Copy did not last. The story of his adoption and Mr. White's plea made the Associated Press wires and newspapers all over the country, but starvation and injury were too much for Copy. He went blind in a few days and a little later went mad. McDaniel, who in addition to being sports editor is the duly elected coroner of Lyon County, Kans., and I took the kitten to the furnace room and put him out of his misery with a bottle of chloroform.

Mr. White's fun with the office gang frequently finds its way into the paper, as, for example, when the following item written by the boss appeared on page 2 of Saturday's noon edition:

"HERE'S YOUR CHANCE

"Mr. and Mrs. W. A. White will spend Sunday with friends in Kansas City, Mo. Mr. and Mrs. Frank Clough and Mr. and Mrs. Wayne Davidson will also be in Kansas City. Mr. Gene Kemper will be in Topeka. Mr. and Mrs. W. L. White are in New York City. So if you are going to have an accident this afternoon, get married, be born, die, or disgrace yourself in any of a lot of interesting ways, here's your chance to get away with it while the *Gazette* boss, the man-

215

aging editor, the business manager, the sports and courthouse reporter all are out of town. This is the devil's own opportunity."

Gazette employees always are going out of town and Mr. White encourages it. That was one of the reasons why he shortened the working week long before the wage and hour law was thought of, so employees could get off early on Saturday for a big week end. So often is someone away that, when Mr. White is gone and writes to the office, he does not always know who will be there to receive his letters. From La Jolla, Calif., a couple of years ago, he wanted me, Gene Lowther, who was advertising manager, or Wayne Davidson, who was business manager, or all of us, to see a letter so he addressed it as follows:

> "Employees of The Gazette
> "Emporia, Kansas,
> "Attention: Frankengenenwayne."

On Mrs. White's last birthday anniversary, she called for Mr. White late in the day and they started home together. At the front door he left her, hurried back, and whispered to me:

"As soon as we are gone, call Ora Rindom, the

216

florist, and tell him to send Mrs. White a dozen big roses with the card reading 'Will A. White.' I've been sending them to her all day from every florist in town. Never had so much fun in my life."

All that day Mrs. White received flowers with cards reading "William Allen White," "Will A. White," "W. Allen White," "William A. White," "The Boss," "Your Husband," and "Guess Who."

The men and women in the *Gazette* never have to account to Mr. White for their time. He trusts them all and knows that the work to be done will be done. His employees come and go as they please, going to the drugstores for drinks during the day or doing personal errands without the boss's paying any attention to them. And the system works. Only a few work when the boss is around and loaf when he is gone, but even they get away with it, for he never says anything. He knows who they are and he probably thinks they go to so much trouble to put on a front when he is around that they are punishing themselves. Only once did I ever hear of his making a remark about an employee not being in the office. One morning he asked where a certain employee was and was told that the man was meeting a train because his girl was going

217

through. The next afternoon Mr. White asked for the same man and was given the same answer.

"What the hell!" he exclaimed. "Is she going through in sections? If he ever gets her all together, I'd like to see what she looks like."

CHAPTER XXI

MARY AND BILL

THE GREATEST TRAGEDY TO BEFALL the family was the sudden death of Mr. and Mrs. White's only daughter, Mary, at the age of sixteen, when her pony ran under a tree and she was struck on the head by a low-hanging limb as she waved at a *Gazette* carrier boy, a high school friend. I knew Mary White for only a year, but it was a year of pleasure and of anxiety for me. While she had a heart of gold and was always ready to do something to help someone who really needed help, she was a fun-loving tomboy and during that year a lot of her fun was had at my expense. When I came to the *Gazette* she spotted me immediately as a bashful person who could be embarrassed easily. Inviting me to the White home for dinner, especially when the family had guests of more or less prominence, was one of her favorite stunts. While she got great enjoyment from my embarrassment, she worked hard to put me at ease and I shall always re-

219

member Mary White as doing more than anyone else to help me to be natural when meeting strangers.

Mary had read all her life—Mark Twain, Dickens, Kipling, and many others of the classics before she was ten years old. The actual work of school was no worry to her, but her school life was a problem because there she found so many ways to have fun that she was a constant worry to her teachers and principals, who felt her antics disrupted the general order of education. When Mary was not at school or at home she was either riding her pony or driving the family's old Dodge touring car. And never did she drive far alone. Nearly everyone she saw walking on the street she picked up until the car was filled. She picked up young and old and black and white. They all looked alike to her and she enjoyed them. Once she found a Negro girl reading in a toilet in the high school because she felt the white girls did not like to have her use the school's only rest room for girls. Immediately Mary set up a howl for a rest room for the colored girls and she hounded school officials for such a room until her death. Afterward the room was supplied and Mrs. White furnished it. Since then the room has been done over at intervals and Mrs. White has seen that it has had proper furnishings.

Boys as boys never worried Mary White and at sixteen she had never had a regular date. A boy in high
school, known by Mary but not a close friend, com-
mitted a theft, ran away from home, and was arrested.
After he pleaded guilty, was sentenced to the reforma-
tory, and paroled, he was shunned by many of the
other students and immediately Mary took his part.
During the last few months of her life she probably
hauled him around in her car more than she did any
other individual and she delighted in filling up the
car with other boys and girls and then picking him
up. The other children knew better than to treat him
badly when Mary was around. The result was that the
boy's trouble was soon forgotten. I often tried to tease
her about her boy friend, but she refused to be teased
and told me much about his troubles and how the
other high school youngsters were not fair to him.

Only a short obituary appeared in the *Gazette* when
Mary White died, but the day following her funeral
Mr. White in a column-long editorial wrote the story
of her life. Written for her friends and Emporians
who knew her, it was filled with names of only local
interest, but the spirit of the piece appealed to everyone who read it and newspapers and magazines all
over the United States copied it. Since that time it has

been published in more than twenty-five different books designed for high school and college reading. The editorial has been reprinted more than anything else Mr. White has written, and requests for copies of it come to the *Gazette* office continually, although it was written nineteen years ago.

"This piece will live longer than anything else I have ever written," said Mr. White recently when we were discussing the many times it had been reprinted in books and magazines. "If I ever have any lasting fame at all, and I doubt if I shall, it will come from this editorial about Mary. How happy she would have been to know that she would live in the hearts of the young people who have read about her in their high school and college textbooks and the papers and magazines that have printed it."

In her early days in high school Mary White was entered as a student at Wellesley College, Wellesley, Mass., to go there in 1922, but her death came more than a year before she finished high school. These facts were told by her father in the editorial "Mary White," and some of the girls in the Wellesley 1926 graduating class read the editorial in a textbook and entered Mary as a member of the class. Mr. and Mrs. White did not know any members of the class and did not know the girls considered Mary as one of them until the spring of graduation, when the Wellesley seniors notified the Whites that the graduation exercises would honor Mary. The class yearbook was dedicated to her memory and Mr. and Mrs. White paid Mary's class assessment for the memorial left to the school by the class.

Mary White's childhood friends have grown up and many have married and gone away, but Mr. and Mrs. White have kept in touch with many of her closest friends, and even now, nearly twenty years after Mary's death, these young people call on the Whites and are heartily welcomed.

W. L. White, who is often called "Young Bill" and who once resented that name because it made him appear as merely a shadow of his famous father, has not exactly followed the path of his father, the editor of the *Gazette*. Although he is a capable editor and a good business manager, Bill sought his fame away from Emporia and the *Gazette*. And now that he has won a wide and good reputation as a columnist, war correspondent, and radio announcer, he should have no reason for not liking the "Young Bill."

Bill did not miss by much being born in the *Gazette* office. In the early days of the White ownership of the paper, Mrs. White worked hard in the office and she had not stopped five years after they bought the paper, when Bill was born. She stopped work shortly before his birth, but she did not stay away after he was born. As an infant Bill was cradled in a clothesbasket while his mother and father worked. Mrs. White continued to help at the office until Mary was born several years later, but the fact that his mother had returned to the home did not keep Bill away. As a child he roamed all over the place, and as soon as he was big enough he began walking around with the carrier boys on their routes. As soon as he was large enough to carry a sack of papers and hit a front porch, he was given a route to carry. As a child Bill had read about everything that was printed—not only the good books in his father's library but even the cheap magazines he and other boys found on the newsstands and read in the barn—and it was only natural that as soon as he was in high school he began to think more of the office than of his paper route. He wrote high school news for the *Gazette* and later became editor of his high school paper. Summers, when he was not away with the family on vacations, he worked in the newspaper office. A year at the University of Kansas, a trip to Europe, four years at Harvard, another trip to Europe,

Mary White, Daughter of Mr. and Mrs. William Allen White,
as She Appeared Shortly before Her Death in 1921.

and then Bill came back to take his place on the *Gazette* staff, arriving in 1924 just after the paper had
started printing two editions a day instead of one. The
early edition, published shortly after noon, was for the
towns in the surrounding territory, and to Bill went
the job of building up the subscription lists in these
towns and in the country. Bill went from door to door
soliciting subscribers and showing his new carriers
how to do the job. He offered prizes to the boys who
did the best job, and soon the *Gazette's* subscription
lists had nearly doubled, with the paper going to towns
in all directions within a radius of fifty miles of Emporia. While Bill was busy building the circulation, I
was working as neighbor-town editor and hiring correspondents. Bill and I together were going into the
small towns to cover more important stories such as
murders, trials, and other events that would add to
the paper's readers. In 1927 at the *Gazette's* annual
Christmas dinner, at which the Whites are hosts to all
Gazette employees, their wives, and their children,
Mr. White announced that Bill was the new associate
editor. For years he had been writing editorials off
and on, many of which were mistaken for the work of
his father, and now Bill was ready to help take some
of the load from his father's shoulders. In 1930 the

225

political bug bit him and he ran and was elected on the Republican ticket to the state legislature from Lyon County. A belief that a state income tax would do a great deal to take the load off real estate and reduce the general property tax led him into the political race and he was one of the leaders in the successful campaign for the new tax, which passed the legislature in 1931. One taste of political office was enough and he did not seek reelection after his first two-year term, but he found a much greater job.

Walter E. Hughes, who was a printer when Mr. White bought the *Gazette* in 1895 and who had risen to business manager and Mr. White's right-hand man, became ill late in the summer of 1932 and died on September 4. Young Bill immediately became business manager of the paper and, much to the surprise of many Emporians, who did not think Bill had paid as much attention to the paper as he should have, he was very successful. The second floor of the *Gazette* building long had been occupied by the Elks Lodge, which for years had been growing poorer. Finally it was about to "fold," and, urged by Bill to find new quarters, the lodge decided to disband. Bill immediately called on architects, engineers, and a rental agent at the same time. Before plans were completed for remodeling the second floor into modern, air-conditioned office rooms—the first in Emporia—the rental agent had signed up doctors and dentists for long leases and then the remodeling project was started. A part of the building, which had paid poorly for years, now proved to be a good investment and Mr. and Mrs. William Allen White were proud of their son's achievement.

In 1934, Bill and his wife, the former Katherine Klinkenberg, whom he had married in 1931 while she was a writer for *Time* magazine in New York, decided to leave Emporia. Going first to Washington and then New York, Bill worked on newspapers and magazines, most of the time writing political news. But he always was seeking something a little different—a job he liked better. During this time he wrote a book, "What People Said," which the author claimed to be purely fictional, but which was based in part on the life of his parents, his own life, and the story of Emporia. The climax of the book was a small-town bond scandal, in which a banker father and his son, an investment broker, became involved to the extent of more than a million dollars. W. W. Finney, who had been a social friend of Mr. White for many years, and his son, Ronald, with whom Young Bill grew up in Emporia, had become involved in such a scandal, the father tak-

227

ing his own life after conviction and sentence for embezzlement, and the son, Ronald, going to the Kansas
penitentiary for a long sentence after pleading guilty
to looting the Kansas state treasury in his bond manip-
ulations. Following publication of his novel, which for
a long time was a best seller, Bill White quit his job
with a magazine and became a free lance writer, doing
articles on social, political, and economic subjects for
magazines. In the summer of 1939 he began writing a
daily column for a New York newspaper and a Midwestern syndicate, much of the time writing of Kansas
and the farm belt. In the fall he sailed for Europe to
continue his daily column from the war zone and,
after a few broadcasts in Germany for the Columbia
Broadcasting chain, he flew to Finland and until
spring continued his writing for his syndicate and his
broadcasting for Columbia. There Young Bill really
won his fame, and, when he returned to the United
States in the summer of 1940, he toured the country
making speeches on general conditions in Europe and
his experiences while reporting war news under fire
in Finland.

Before Bill returned home, a motion picture newsreel of shots in Finland, showing Bill in the war zone,
was released in the United States and was shown for

four days in Emporia. The first night Mr. and Mrs. William Allen White went to the first show, saw the newsreel, the feature, and the newsreel again. The next night at dinner they both announced at the same time they again would like to see the picture, which showed such brief shots of their son. With a party of guests, who had not seen the picture, they went to the seven o'clock show, saw the newsreel, and returned home. I took them home and hurried back to see the feature, but at nine o'clock I returned to the White home, asked Mr. and Mrs. White if they would not like to drive down to see the newsreel again, and was not at all surprised when they quickly agreed. The next night they again saw the picture twice and the fourth night they returned for one showing. This was not funny to Emporians, who knew the love and hope the Whites held for their only living child, and everyone who knew of the incident seemed to understand. In fact, many of Young Bill's friends paid to see the newsreel more than once. The Whites, incidentally, merely walked in on their annual passes.

Following his lecture tour in the summer and early fall of 1940, Bill again became interested in the war, with London as his particular interest. He knew he could never again get into Germany, Italy, or Russia, because of things he had written and broadcast about those countries, so he made plans for the next trip to be confined to England. Signed up with another syndicate and a magazine, he sailed again in the fall of 1940, making the trip to England on one of the American destroyers the United States traded to Great Britain for naval bases in a deal urged by William Allen White's Committee to Defend America by Aiding the Allies. The circumstances of the sailing have never been divulged, but Mr. White seemed as surprised as anyone else when Young Bill telephoned from New York to Emporia to announce that he was going over on one of the United States' outmoded boats. Bill undoubtedly used his father's name in pulling wires to get this ride, but I am sure his father had nothing to do with the arrangements. Newspaper stories at intervals and a few broadcasts kept Young Bill busy until late in January, when he again sailed for the United States to write another book and to give another series of lectures.

CHAPTER XXII

GAZETTE ALUMNI

TO TELL ABOUT WILLIAM ALLEN WHITE without telling something about some of the men who have worked for him—who got their starts in the world with him—would be leaving out an important part of his life, for he never forgets a man who has worked for the *Gazette*. Most widely known of all these men, probably, was Walt Mason, who wrote hundreds and hundreds of poems for newspapers and magazines before his death at his home in La Jolla, Calif., in 1939.

Born in Columbus, Ont., on May 4, 1862, the fifth in a series of six boys in the family, Walt Mason started to school as other children did, but he did not get far. He violently hated everything but the readers in the Canadian schools and arithmetic completely baffled him. He studied the readers over and over and later said that some of the poems took such complete possession of him that he could think of nothing else for days. So his school days ended early, with Walt Mason as glad to get out of classes as his teachers were to see him go. For years after quitting school he worked on farms, clerked in stores, fed presses in printing offices, and did many other jobs to earn enough for something to eat and a place to sleep while he went through life enjoying nothing except the poetry he read. His first writing job was about 1884 for the *Atchison* (Kans.) *Globe,* when the late Ed Howe, "The Sage of Potato Hill," gave Mason a job as a reporter. That job Mason liked and he specialized in writing local news—the doings of the Atchison people. Leaving Atchison, he went to the *State Journal* in Lincoln, Neb., and there he became acquainted with William Jennings Bryan, Charles G. Dawes, and "Black Jack" Pershing, later commander of the United States forces in the First World War. From Lincoln he went to the *Omaha World-Herald* and then to a new paper, the *Evening News* in Washington, D. C., where he gained his first fame when he wrote a notable piece on the death of James G. Blaine.

For a time Mason rode high as a Washington newspaperman, but in the panic of 1893 he lost his job and returned to Nebraska. While in Washington he had married Ella Foos, of Wooster, Ohio, and together they returned to Nebraska, where things went from bad to worse for them. As things got worse, Mason began drinking, and the worse they got, the more he drank. Three times he took the Keeley cure for liquor, but each time he went back to it. Finally Mrs. Mason went home to live with her parents and Mason loaded his only possessions—one valise of clothing and a battered typewriter—into an old buckboard drawn by a pinto pony and started on the road. His quest for a job brought him to Emporia, a man about forty-five years old, broke financially and broken spiritually. Mr. White looked him over, liked him immediately, hired him as a reporter, and gave him a battered old desk to match the battered old typewriter. In Emporia Mason took a new interest in life. He liked to write better than any other man who had been on the *Gazette* staff and Mr. White encouraged him. Completely taken by his work, he forgot drink and soon was able to send for Mrs. Mason. One busy Saturday, Mason wrote in prose form a rhyme urging people to go to church the next day. Emporians read it and the churches were filled. Monday Mr. White suggested Mason write another prose poem and from then on they were daily features. Although the subject matter generally was of only local interest, Mason's manner of expression appealed to other editors and soon his poems were being copied by many other papers. Mr. White, realizing that Mason was doing something for which he should receive more money, wrote to George Matthew Adams, who had a syndicate, and Adams immediately began selling Mason's daily verse under the title of "Rippling Rhymes" by "Uncle Walt."

From then on the Masons enjoyed life, but "Uncle Walt" never enjoyed popularity. He shunned parties of all kinds and lived to himself and his family. The Masons adopted a daughter and built a fine home in Emporia, which Mason paid for as it went up. The more money the builder said he needed for men and materials, the more Mason wrote, and at one time he was doing his daily syndicate rhymes, six prose stories a week for the *Chicago News,* a Sunday story for the *Kansas City Star,* twenty rhymes a week for trade papers, a rhyme a month for *Judge,* and many others.

Mason never returned to liquor and he was happy in Emporia, except for the cold winters. The family began going to California for the cold weather and gradually they began going earlier and staying later each year. In 1920 they announced that La Jolla was their permanent home and the possessions in Emporia were sold. There "Uncle Walt" lived by the sea and continued to turn out poems in mass production. Mason continually shunned invitations to return to Emporia, because he knew Emporians would "make a fuss" over him and he would have to go to parties. Not until 1938—two years after Mrs. Mason had died—did Mason and his daughter, Mary, and their dog come to Emporia, and that time no one knew anything about the visit until they drove up in front of the *Gazette* office in a big black car with all the modern gadgets they could hang on it. They remained in Emporia several weeks and never once went to a party or accepted a dinner invitation. "Uncle Walt" spent most of his time walking the streets and renewing his old acquaintances, or sitting in his hotel room reading and entertaining visitors he called in one at a time.

In 1939 Mason died, a man of seventy-seven who had made a success of life after forty-five and who before that age had fallen low. He was only one of the men who was started on the road to success by the editor of *The Emporia Gazette,* but Mason became one of the best known and his case is unusual because of the depths to which he fell before he became successful.

All over the country in all lines of work are successful men who got their start on the *Gazette.* Natu-

235

rally a majority of them are in newspaper work, but there are many others.

Brock Pemberton, one of Broadway's noted play producers, started his life as a newspaperman and got his first "yen" for the stage while he was a reporter for *The Emporia Gazette*. All of Pemberton's mother's family were newspaper people and it was only natural that they should have picked that life for him. Upon his graduation from Emporia High School in 1902, he was given his first job on the *Gazette* and, after attending College of Emporia and finishing at Kansas University in 1908, he returned to Emporia as a regular reporter. At that time the only big auditorium in Emporia was at the old Kansas Normal School, now Kansas State Teachers College, and Frank A. Beach, head of the school's music department, was the man who handled Emporia's theatricals. Beach booked the shows, making money on some and losing on others, but he kept a jack pot that made the paying ones make up the deficits of those that lost. In that way, Emporia constantly got good attractions even though some of the better things did not make expenses. Beach, who had a natural eye for good things on the stage as well as an ear for music, took an interest in Pemberton when the young reporter began writing publicity and reviews of the stage shows. Later when Pemberton went to New York to continue his newspaper career, it was natural that he should continue his leaning toward the theater and become a critic.

Arthur Hopkins, New York producer, was attracted by both Pemberton and his reviews and took the Kansan into his office as an assistant. When a play, "Enter Madame," was offered to Hopkins and he decided not to take it, Pemberton asked permission to do the show and he did it with success. Since then he has been putting shows on New York stages and on road tours, a few of which have reached Emporia. The high point in Pemberton's career probably was in 1921 when he was given the Pulitzer award for his production of Zona Gale's "Miss Lulu Bett," but, as far as Emporia is concerned, Pemberton's big moment was Apr. 16, 1936, when he came here and made a personal appearance with his comedy, "Personal Appearance," which he presented with the original New York cast. All seats were one dollar for adults and fifty cents for students. More than two thousand persons crowded into the school auditorium, where Pemberton always before had appeared as a spectator and critic, and Mr. and Mrs. White were among those in the first few rows. When Pemberton made his curtain

237

speech, the crowd stood and applauded another *Gazette* reporter who had gone out and made good and Editor White beamed like a boy with a new bicycle.

Murdock Pemberton, a brother of Brock, who also went to New York, is another former *Gazette* reporter who has gained note, but not by staying with a newspaper. Murdock went to New York to do publicity and in a few years was in charge of the press bureau of William A. Brady, producer. He has continued in writing, however, and his work appears frequently in magazines.

All over the country, men who started as boys on the *Gazette* are working for newspapers, and many of them are owners. A typical career is that of Oscar Stauffer.

Needing a high school reporter in 1906, Mr. White telephoned the high school and asked the principal to send him over a boy who might make a reporter.

"I want one who doesn't smoke, swear, and probably won't grow up to drink," the editor said. Principal C. H. Lyon called young Oscar Stauffer to his office, told him of the call, and sent him to the *Gazette* office after school. The boy got the job and stayed until he finished high school, in 1908. Later Stauffer attended the University of Kansas and then got a job as a reporter for the *Kansas City Star,* where he worked for five years, until 1915, when he went to Peabody, Kans., and bought a weekly paper. In 1924 he sold at Peabody and bought the *Daily Traveler* at Arkansas City, Kans., a few years later buying the competing *Daily News* and merging it with his *Traveler.* From then on Stauffer climbed in the newspaper business. Today he owns the *Arkansas City Traveler,* the *Topeka State Journal* and the *Pittsburg Morning Sun* and *Evening Headlight,* all in Kansas, the *Daily Independent* at Grand Island, Neb., the *Morning News* and *Evening Star* at Shawnee, Okla., and the *Evening Forum* at Maryville, Mo. And Stauffer is only one of many men who are proud that they were first employed by William Allen White on *The Emporia Gazette.*

CHAPTER XXIII

A CONSTANT WRITER

IN ADDITION TO MOST OF THE EDITO-
rials which have appeared in the *Gazette* every day
in the forty-five years Mr. White has owned it, he has
written hundreds of news stories for newspaper syn-
dicates, as well as thousands for his own paper. He has
written many magazine articles and sixteen books. His
first book, "The Real Issue," a collection of short
stories which was published in 1896, the year after he
bought the *Gazette,* sold widely, probably because the
book came close on the heels of the editorial "What's
the Matter with Kansas?" which won the editor his
first national recognition. "The Real Issue" was a
group of short stories that had accumulated over several years, some of them having been published pre-
viously in the *El Dorado Republican,* in the *Kansas
City Star* and in the *Gazette.*

Another collection of short stories, "The Court of
Boyville," was published in 1899, followed in 1901 by

240

The Editor Pauses as He Signs His Daily Mail.

another collection, "Stratagems and Spoils." In 1906 came another collection, "In Our Town," and his first novel, "A Certain Rich Man," came out in 1909.

Having saved a little money and worked hard on the novel, Mr. White felt that he and Mrs. White and their two children, Bill, who was nine, and Mary, five, needed a vacation and they went to Europe right after the book was published, without knowing how the public accepted it. After resting and touring, during which they received only meager news from America, the Whites started home, still not knowing whether "A Certain Rich Man" had been a success or a flop. Boarding a boat for the trip home, Mrs. White saw a man in a deck chair reading a copy of the *New York Times,* the outside page of which carried an advertisement with big letters reading, "A Certain Rich Man." So excited she could hardly talk, she interrupted and asked if she could borrow the paper when the man had finished. Then they waited and to them it seemed that never before did a man read a paper so long. Finally he finished and the Whites grabbed the paper and rushed to their cabin, where alone they read that the book was a great success.

"I was so happy that I cried and I know Will shed some tears," says Mrs. White, who still is proud and thrilled at each new accomplishment of her husband. "The children couldn't understand it when we explained we were happy. To them tears were another story."

"The Old Order Changeth," a book of political essays, came out in 1910, followed by another collection of short stories, "God's Puppets," in 1916. After Mr. White returned from Europe where, in 1917, he went with Henry J. Allen, Wichita, Kans., editor, as officers of the American Red Cross to study the war situation, he wrote "The Martial Adventures of Henry and Me," which was half novel and half travel sketches. His second novel, "In the Heart of a Fool," published in 1918, was his last and he turned to more serious affairs. He wrote "Woodrow Wilson, the Man, the Times, and His Task," published in 1924, and that same year he did "Politics, the Citizen's Business." "Calvin Coolidge, the Man Who Is President," came out in 1925, and in 1928, "Masks in a Pageant," a book of sketches of the presidents from McKinley through Coolidge, and of certain contemporary statesmen, was published. The story of the 1936 presidential campaign, "What It's All About," was published that year, and in 1938, "A Puritan in Babylon," the story of Calvin Coolidge, was printed. Off and on, Mr.

White spent about ten years on this story and he did a great deal of research as well as travel to get the facts. His latest book, "The Changing West," telling of the characteristics of the West and its influence on American life and philosophy, came out in 1939.

Mr. White has several things "on the fire" now, but he is not close to the publishing stage of anything. How soon he might bring out something else could be only a guess, for almost any day he may start to work on something in earnest. On the other hand, he might start something and find many interruptions, as was the case with his last Coolidge story, which was not finally finished and "okayed" by him until long after his publishers had been promised it. Someday he hopes to publish his autobiography, but it, too, is something in the offing; no one knows how far.

"I've been going to do it for years," he told me when I asked him about it before writing this piece, "but when I'll ever get it done is hard to tell. I've even promised it to a publisher, but I may never do it."

To Mr. and Mrs. White, home means more than anything else in the world and they are sincere in it to the extent that they probably stay in their own home more than anyone else in Emporia. They have guests for dinner or an evening ten to one more times than they go out and they entertain out-of-town guests much more than they are guests of someone else. Neither of them likes to be long away from home, but neither likes to be away from the other. For that reason, Mrs. White usually accompanies Mr. White on his business trips East several times a year and on shorter trips. Only when it is absolutely necessary that they be separated does one go away without the other and then telegrams and telephone calls fly thick and fast. To them home is a place to enjoy and they enjoy it together, naturally and easily.

Always Mr. and Mrs. White are up together by seven o'clock or earlier in the morning and they have breakfast together. Either Mrs. White or Miss Colglazier, their housekeeper, takes Mr. White to the office before eight o'clock and he never fails to kiss Mrs. White good-by before he leaves the house. Always, except on Rotary Club days or other special occasions when Mr. White has to stay downtown for luncheon, he goes home at noon and often as early as eleven or eleven thirty he calls the house for Mrs. White or Miss Colglazier to come for him. When he has to stay downtown for luncheon, he goes home immediately afterward and for years he has taken a nap of from an hour to an hour and a half, always retiring to his bedroom and usually taking off most of his clothes and donning a robe or pajamas. By two thirty or three o'clock he is back at the office again, looking over and answering the afternoon mail, reading the papers from other towns that have come in since he was there in the morning, reading the first edition of his own paper, or writing editorials for the next day. About four thirty or five o'clock Mrs. White comes for him in the car or he rides home with someone from the office. Never does he work at night.

"Don't work at night," he told me, when I told him I was writing this piece at home nights. "A long time ago I worked at the office all day and wrote at home at night and I nearly had a nervous breakdown. I had to quit work and take a long rest and it cost me more in the end than it was worth. Don't try to work all day at the office and then write at home at night. It'll kill you."

Mr. White's working day always is about the same length. The difference is that when he is writing a book, a magazine article, or a speech, he works faster. Frequently when he is doing these things, he hurries to the office in the morning, dictates his editorials and answers urgent mail, and then takes his secretary home with him for dictation in his study until noon. Often

245

he has his secretary come to the house in the afternoon, but nearly always he shows up himself at the office in the afternoon, if only for a few minutes. He does some of his work at home, especially if he is working hard and is pressed for time, because there few persons bother him. At the office he is constantly interrupted by people coming in to see him about this or that, and many take their news items to him, even though most of them know he will usher them into the newsroom and turn them over to someone else. But he enjoys seeing all these people.

Mr. White's general office at the *Gazette* is a small room between the business office and the newsroom, with doors entering from both. Reporters, advertising men, bookkeepers, and all the rest form a constant parade through his office, even when he has visitors, although a hallway runs the entire length of the *Gazette* building and it is only a little longer through the plant that way. But Mr. White encourages his employees to take the short cut through his office. Once I started through, noticed that he was having an earnest conversation with an important visitor who I did not know was in town, and I apologized quietly and started back.

"Wait a minute," he called to me. "You don't need

to apologize for going through here. That's what these doors are for and I want you to go through. You don't bother me any. I like it."

In another part of the building, just a few steps from the news office and in an air-conditioned wing of the *Gazette* building which also is occupied by a doctor's suite, Mr. White has a small office which once was private, but which now is known by about everyone. The door between the office and the newsroom has a sign reading "Private" and another door separates Mr. White's little office from the hall. The "Private" sign is to keep outsiders from invading this little office, which is the one place in the building where Mr. White can hide out. But he does not hide from *Gazette* employees. When he first began using this office—and he seldom uses it at all—a printer with a handful of editorial proofs for the boss stopped at the door and knocked. A few minutes later, while the proofs waited, Mr. White was placing on the door a cardboard sign reading, *"Gazette* Employees Enter without Knocking." But Mr. White does not like this private office because he feels that it keeps him away from things. For years and years he has worked where he could hear the clicking of the linotypes, the whirr

247

of motors, the roar from the pressroom, and the clatter and conversation in the news and business offices.

I never enter this private office but I remember one busy morning three or four years ago when Mr. White walked through the newsroom, motioned for me to follow him, and led the way into the little air-conditioned room.

"I don't have anything much special on my mind," he announced when we had been seated. "I just wanted to talk to you. I guess I just wanted to tell you this: If ever I get so that I can't do a decent day's work, will you do me a favor? I want you to get a good-sized club and put me out of my misery. That's all."

What had happened before, I never found out. But I have never felt that the time had arrived for me to get the club, and I do not believe it ever will. The boss can still do as big a day's work as any man in the place and I believe he always will until he quits for good. He will stay in the harness until his name is called.

CHAPTER XXIV

IN CONCLUSION

I DON'T THINK MR. WHITE IS APPRE-
ciated here," I have heard many Emporians say.
"When I go away and people find out I am from
Emporia, they always say, 'That's where William Allen White lives.' You have to get away from Emporia
to realize how big a man Mr. White really is."

Such an observation is partly right. While Mr.
White and his national prominence are definitely ap-
preciated in Emporia, his fellow townsmen have become accustomed to him. And that is the way he wants
it. First of all, Mr. White is an Emporian—the editor
of the local newspaper. He walks down the street as
other men do, he shops in the stores, he is not above
taking home a pound of butter or head of lettuce that
might have been overlooked when the day's grocery
order was telephoned, he goes to the local civic meetings, and he sits in the movie among his friends and
subscribers. The fact that he has written books, that

249

he is a leader in national affairs, that he is a friend of Presidents, that prominent men from far and wide seek his home and his office—these things have not gone to his head and taken his mind from Emporia.

Emporians know that many times the country editor has had attractive offers to go to larger cities to fill private or public positions that the average man would not turn down. But because he has stayed at home and insisted on being an Emporian at heart as well as from outward appearances, Emporians have never treated him in any other way than as one of them.

Many other men can write as well as Mr. White can and many have gained more fame as writers. Great numbers of men have just as fine character as Mr. White has. In political talent he does not stand out alone. The world is full of humanitarians such as he, seeking no rewards for themselves.

"Then why," you may ask, "is Mr. White the remarkable national figure he is?"

I have thought of this hundreds of times during the twenty years I have been with Mr. White. But I can find no better answer than the explanation given by Harry Norton, local cleaner and presser, in whose shop Mr. White often stops to visit.

"Your boss is a remarkable man," said Norton.

"There are a lot of men who can do some of the things he does just as well and some can do them better. But there aren't many who can do all the things he can and do them as well. And when you can find a man who has all the ability and qualities Mr. White has and who could get as far personally as he could, but who would rather be known first as editor of a country-town paper, you let me know. Then I'll show you a man who might be as great as I think Mr. White is."

I think Mr. White would be more genuinely pleased at such a tribute from Harry Norton, a fellow Emporian, than he would with a precious medal or national recognition from someone who knew him less well. That, in my opinion, is why Mr. White truly is a great man.

INDEX

A

Abolitionists, 44, 50
Admire, Kans., 201
Alexander, C. C., 138
Allen, Henry, 170-173, 180
American Red Cross, 180
American Society of Newspaper Editors, 26
Arkansas City (Kans.) *Daily Traveler,* 239
Associated Press, 10, 12, 183, 193
Atchison (Kans.) *Globe,* 232
Augusta, 37-40
Automobiles, 203-205

B

Bargains, 136-142
Beach, Frank A., 236

Beer in Kansas, 165-168
Belgium, 11, 178
Bingham, Barry, 193
Blaine, James G., 232
Book of the Month Club, 9, 14, 212
Bootlegging, 165
Brady, William A., 238
Broadview Hotel, 151-153
Brogan, J. C., 123
Bryan, William Jennings, 144, 232
Business, White's views on, 134-142
Butler County, 36, 41
Butler County Democrat, 61

C

Capper, Senator Arthur, 119
Carnegie, Andrew, 186

254

INDEX

255

INDEX

INDEX

White, William Allen (Cont.)
printer, work as, 17, 18, 28-33, 55, 57
prohibitionist, 163-168
Pulitzer prize editorial (1922), 173-175
reading, 45, 51, 52, 56
red tie, 20
reporting, reminiscences of, 59-64
Republican party, work for, 147, 148
Rotary Club (*see* Rotary Club)
shopping expeditions, 135-137
working day, 244, 245
writings, 240-243
books, 240-243
editorials (*see* Editorials)
news stories, 111, 213, 240
poetry, 31-33
"Y," campaign to save, 125-133
(*See also* Committee to Defend America by Aiding the Allies; Re-

publican party; *The Emporia Gazette*)
White, Mrs. William Allen (Sallie Lindsay), 52, 57, 60, 65-67, 71, 72, 97, 98, 166, 167, 173, 183, 203-206, 212
birthday, 216, 217
employees' families, interest in, 101-103, 225
Gazette, influence on, 104, 105
news items for, 106, 107
writings for, 104, 105
illness, 192
park memorial and, 115-124
Republican, 147
trips, 244
"Y," work for, 127
"Young Bill's" broadcasts and, 207, 228, 229
White, William L. ("Young Bill"), 30, 156, 203, 215, 223-230
broadcasts war news, 105, 207, 208, 228-230
column, 228